Museums and Millennials

AMERICAN ASSOCIATION FOR STATE AND LOCAL HISTORY BOOK SERIES

ABOUT THE SERIES

The American Association for State and Local History Book Series addresses issues critical to the field of state and local history through interpretive, intellectual, scholarly, and educational texts. To submit a proposal or manuscript to the series, please request proposal guidelines from AASLH headquarters: AASLH Editorial Board, 2021 21st Ave. South, Suite 320, Nashville, Tennessee 37212. Telephone: (615) 320-3203. Website: www.aaslh.org.

ABOUT THE ORGANIZATION

The American Association for State and Local History (AASLH) is a national history membership association headquartered in Nashville, Tennessee, that provides leadership and support for its members who preserve and interpret state and local history in order to make the past more meaningful to all people. AASLH members are leaders in preserving, researching, and interpreting traces of the American past to connect the people, thoughts, and events of yesterday with the creative memories and abiding concerns of people, communities, and our nation today. In addition to sponsorship of this book series, AASLH publishes *History News* magazine, a newsletter, technical leaflets and reports, and other materials; confers prizes and awards in recognition of outstanding achievement in the field; supports a broad education program and other activities designed to help members work more effectively; and advocates on behalf of the discipline of history. To join AASLH, go to www.aaslh.org or contact Membership Services, AASLH, 2021 21st Ave. South, Suite 320, Nashville, TN 37212.

Museums and Millennials

Engaging the Coveted Patron Generation

JACLYN SPAINHOUR

ROWMAN & LITTLEFIELD
Lanham • Boulder • New York • London

Published by Rowman & Littlefield
A wholly owned subsidiary of The Rowman & Littlefield Publishing Group, Inc.
4501 Forbes Boulevard, Suite 200, Lanham, Maryland 20706
www.rowman.com

Unit A, Whitacre Mews, 26-34 Stannary Street, London SE11 4AB

British Library Cataloguing in Publication Information Available

Library of Congress Cataloging-in-Publication Data Available

ISBN: 978-1-5381-1857-3 (cloth : alk. paper)
ISBN: 978-1-5381-1858-0 (pbk. : alk. paper)
ISBN: 978-1-5381-1859-7 (electronic)

∞™ The paper used in this publication meets the minimum requirements of
American National Standard for Information Sciences—Permanence of Paper
for Printed Library Materials, ANSI/NISO Z39.48-1992.

Contents

Preface

*M*USEUMS *and Millennials: Engaging the Coveted Patron Generation* is intended as a resource for small and mid-sized museums to aid staff in the creation, revision, and implementation of programming geared toward a millennial audience. This book is organized thematically by key concepts including defining the millennial audience, affordability, uniqueness, relevance, accessibility, and envisioning the museum of the future. Each chapter is designed to provide insight into how museum professionals can identify, reach, and engage a millennial audience. This is the first work to focus solely on engaging this coveted patron generation in the museum world. This subject as a point of scholarly research is in its infancy, which means there are limited resources available for museum professionals to draw upon. The available source material for this book includes limited data sets, primary and secondary print materials, and author-conducted interviews of museum professionals and industry leaders. *Museums and Millennials* is set apart due to its innovative methodological approach and use of real-life examples of successful and unsuccessful millennial-geared programming used at museums and cultural institutions across the country. Readers will walk away from this book inspired to reassess the programs at their respective institutions and safe in the knowledge that millennials value museums and are seeking the experiences they offer.

This work is meant to act as a springboard for museum professionals to begin the conversations needed to revamp their programming to reach newer, younger audiences, rather than a comprehensive "how-to" book to reach millennials as a homogenous patron group. The purpose of this book is not to help museum professionals replace their current patron groups, but to add on to them by reaching a millennial audience. The information in this book is based on the personal experiences of the author, as well as the experiences of various museum professionals representing different museums across the country. The staff sizes, budget constraints, governing organizations, and report gathering methods also differ among the participating museum representatives. For this reason, more data and insight may be available only for certain events featured in this work. Overall, the examples used will offer insight into how programs may be adapted to reach this millennial audience and inspire museum professionals to think creatively when crafting programming to complement their collections and mission statements.

Chapter 1 introduces the reader to the millennial generation using statistics and data sets to debunk the myths surrounding millennial attitudes purported by society at large in an effort to redefine the millennial as a worthy patron group. This chapter discusses who millennials are, who they are not, what current literature says about them, why museums should market to millennials, defines the types of millennial audiences, and informs the reader of how this book will help them reach this audience.

Chapters 2 through 5 provide the content chapters for the Affordability, Uniqueness, Relevance, and Accessibility (A.U.R.A.) self-assessment. Chapter 2 covers affordability by defining millennial incomes, spending habits, views on admission prices, and how museum professionals can design affordable programs for their facilities. Chapter 3 describes uniqueness by defining what uniqueness means to millennials in terms of programming, why millennials value innovation, and how museum professionals can create unique programs. Chapter 4 focuses on relevance by defining the term for a millennial audience and discussing the importance of aligning programming with the museum's mission. Chapter 5 discusses accessibility by defining the term for a millennials audience and discussing how to manage millennial expectations. Each chapter provides a breakdown in a section called "practical applications" that explains how these concepts relate to the millennial subgroups. Each chapter also features examples of programs implemented at museums across the country geared toward a millennial audience with suggestions of how readers might use those examples in their own facilities.

Chapter 6 offers readers a glimpse into the future with millennials at the helm in the museum world. The chapter advocates for millennials in the boardroom, as donors, as members, as patrons, as volunteers, as interns, and as senior staff.

Readers are sure to come away from this book with a renewed excitement and determination to succeed in engaging a millennial audience. In order to build a solid foundation for museums to succeed in the future, it is imperative that museum professionals start having these conversations focused on the millennial audience, who will serve as the donors, members, trustees, volunteers, and museum professionals of the future. Millennial engagement should be on the top of all priority lists for museum professionals seeking growth and stability for the future of their institutions. This work will help start that conversation.

Acknowledgments

THE idea for this book came to me on a beautiful autumn day as I walked my son around the neighborhood in his little stroller. It was a divine stroke of luck. As I turned a corner, suddenly the concept of A.U.R.A. popped into my head as if it was just waiting to be accessed. I spent the next thirty minutes outlining in my mind what would become the chapters of this book. By some miracle, the good folks at AASLH thought it was worthy of publication and sent it off to Rowman & Littlefield. The rest, as they say, is history.

Anyone who says writing a book is a solo effort is neglecting the aid of the many people who help make their dreams a reality, and I could never suggest the ideas in this book all came from my own noggin. It was the many interviews I conducted, casual conversations I had, and late-night research efforts I made that helped shape the path of this book.

First and foremost, I have to thank Bob Beatty at AASLH for advocating for this project when it was only an idea on paper, and the decision makers at AASLH for believing in its value. I must also thank my editor, Charles Harmon, and his team, for their guidance, constructive criticism, and oversight throughout this process. Thank you for your patience as I worked and reworked parts of this manuscript and for helping me give it life.

This book and its contents would be quite barren without the contributions of the many museum leaders who allowed me to literally air their dirty laundry for the greater good. I cannot possibly thank the following people enough for their honesty and willingness to be featured in this work: Jennifer Lucy of the Hermitage Museum and Gardens, Andy Hahn of the Campbell House Museum, Arlene Marcionette of the Mystic Seaport Museum, Kathy Alcaine of Maymont Mansion, Matt Davis of Georgia College's Historic Houses, Jill Hartz of the Jordan Schnitzer Museum of Art, Meagan Douglas of the Chrysler Museum of Art, Anne Holst of Clouds Hill Victorian House Museum, Christina Shutt of the Mosaic Templars Cultural Association, and others who gave of their time but were not included in the final revisions of this work. Interviews with Dustin Growick of Museum Hack and Colleen Dilenschneider of IMPACTS Research and Development provided much-needed viewpoints from industry leaders to support the ideas in this book. I could not have proceeded without their encouragement that I was on the right track or without the help of the many authors and researchers who came before me who discussed the millennial generation. The research efforts of the Pew Research Center have proven invaluable in validating some of my key concepts regarding millennial trends and mindsets. The opinions in this book are only as good as the research available to support them, and I am delighted there were so many resources at my disposal. Thank you to Morven Moeller for providing fun and engaging illustrations for this book.

Thank you to my millennial friends and to the complete strangers who took the various surveys and answered the random questions I posed both in person and through social media. Your insight has colored the pages of this book in more ways than words can express. Special thanks to Joshua Weinstein, Raven Hudson, Michaela Francis, and Anna Barbay for allowing me to print their quotations in this work. Thank you to my museum colleagues in the South Hampton Roads Museum Forum who helped me troubleshoot when I was stuck, and who encouraged me every step of the way.

Perhaps most importantly, I cannot adequately express my gratitude to my colleagues Raven Hudson and Renee Evans for reading various drafts of this book, always being willing to share their thoughts and ideas as fellow millennials, and for generally putting up with me during the process. You both have been my sounding boards and I am eternally grateful for your support of this work. Carol Naumann and Gloria Eatroff spent countless hours lovingly scrutinizing my work, and for that I am eternally grateful, as well. Thank you to my board of directors for allowing me to spend time working on this project and for always supporting my efforts as a museum professional. Your confidence in me continues to provide fuel for my millennial ambition to change the world.

They may not ever see this, or even know who I am, but I would be remiss not to thank the good people at Cure Coffeehouse in downtown Norfolk for providing the copious amounts of caffeine it required for me to finish this book. The majority of this project was completed at your wooden tables with the aid of lavender mochas and chai tea lattes. Thank you for providing an ambience conducive to creativity, and for always being willing to let people like me sit for hours on end to create something beautiful. You guys rock.

Finally, thank you to my incredibly supportive husband David, who often watched our little toddler so I could work on this book. Without your encouragement, I do not know if this would have ever come to fruition. You believed in this project from the beginning, and for your unwavering confidence in me, I can never repay you. And for my baby Declan, I hope this book helps the next generation of museum leaders make an inclusive museum world for you and others like you with autism spectrum disorder. You all deserve to have these experiences, and I am so proud to have played a small part in helping the movement along.

Thank you, everyone, for your support and encouragement. This book is for you.

1

"Why Millennials?"

I N this chapter, I will introduce you to the generation known as millennials by highlighting the qualities associated with their age group that are relevant to museums and encouraging millennial engagement. I will introduce you to the common misconceptions regarding millennials and explain why it is important that museum professionals ignore those characterizations. I will clearly define who millennials are and what they value when determining how to allocate their time and assets.

In an effort to make you familiar with the analyses that already exist regarding the millennial generation, I will also include a brief overview of scholarly literature concerned with defining millennials and marketing to them. Then, I will discuss why it is vital that museums reach out to and obtain a millennial audience. I will use various limited sets of data to illustrate the buying power of this generation, as well as how their interests demonstrate a natural affinity toward relationships with museums.

Subsequently, I will discuss which types of millennials, based on personality and spending habits, museum directors should take notice of when planning programming at their facilities. This section will focus on subgroups of millennials, which have been defined by scholars in various ways since the 1970s.

After reading this chapter, you should feel comfortable identifying who millennials are and who they are not, what current literature has to say about them, why museum professionals need to reach a millennial audience, and in which millennial subgroups museum staff should take an interest. All of this information will help your staff move forward in implementing the self-assessment offered by the A.U.R.A. checklist and get your facility on its way to gaining a loyal, engaged millennial audience.

WHO ARE MILLENNIALS (AND WHO ARE THEY NOT)?

The front cover of the May 2013 edition of *Time* magazine best characterizes public perception of this generation perfectly with the title, "The Me Me Me Generation: Millennials are Lazy, Entitled Narcissists Who Still Live with Their Parents—Why They'll Save Us All."[1] Millennials are commonly viewed as the "me" generation concerned with their own happiness, marked by rampant narcissism, and possessing a group-wide feeling of entitlement.[2] It is said their childhood development played out like an episode of the *Oprah Winfrey Show*, "You get a trophy! And you get a trophy! And you!" They are viewed as the generation turning away from the tradition of the nine-to-five workday in favor of telecommuting and flex-time positions. They "are the first 'digital natives' and experience the world in a completely different way than previous generations."[3] The public believes they are more likely to hold a protest than run for office. They reject labels yet fight battles behind banners for social and civil rights. Millennials, it seems, are somewhat of a walking paradox, and public perception is not helping society to understand millennial personalities and habits. Thanks to outdated perceptions and biases woven into the generational narrative, determining who they are and what they truly value has been difficult for museum professionals. Perhaps this is why conclusive findings regarding this generation are so hard to find in print.

One of the, if not the, largest problems for staff at museums and cultural institutions seeking to engage this demographic has been determining the answer to this basic question: Who are millennials, really? When consulting various sources of information about millennials, researchers will discover more than half a dozen different definitions of the age range for individuals who qualify to be labeled millennial, along with many competing descriptions of their personalities and values. As we know, if we want to reach this audience, we first need to be able to define them.

Up until recently, the date range for who makes up this generation was much larger than the currently accepted range. The most reliable sources for defining this group have historically come from entities like the Pew Research Center and sociology scholars who specialize in generational identity. The Pew Research Center is responsible for putting forth the most currently accepted date range, noting millennials as anyone born between 1981 and 1996.[4] Previously, the most widely held definition of millennials was individuals who "came of age" with the new millennium, and therefore were born around the early eighties.[5] Other sources suggest birthdate ranges which begin anywhere between 1977 and 1985 and end between 1995 and 2003.[6] With such a disparity present in defining birth date ranges for millennials, it is easy to understand why the thought of marketing to this generation often creates anxiety and panic.

There is also the added issue that a significant segment of the population identified chronologically by these sources as millennials do not self-identify as part of the millennial generation, primarily because they do not wish to be defined by the personality traits prescribed by society to the millennial generation.[7] Those technically classified as older millennials often choose to identify as part of generation X in an attempt to separate themselves from the hallmark characteristics ascribed to millennials by much older generations and popular culture itself: laziness, entitlement, narcissism, and so on. This group of millennials is often identified as "xennials" and reports show as many as 43 percent of millennials consider themselves part of generation X.[8]

Even those who fall perfectly within the date range shy away from owning the label. Part of the reason for this is millennials are a generation uninterested in being defined on any level by any labels. They are less likely to define themselves politically and spiritually, with the majority reporting themselves as not identifying with any major religious group and simultaneously describing themselves as politically independent, although studies show most millennials report liberal leanings.[9] This may also be one of the major reasons why millennials are very accepting of other cultures and often embrace them at a level far above their parents' or grandparents' generation.[10] In fact, 43 percent of the reported millennial generation are non-whites.[11] Many millennials come from racially and ethnically diverse backgrounds, are part of nontraditional families, or work nontraditional jobs.[12] In a way, millennials fight against being defined in all aspects of their lives.

In accordance with the Pew Research Center, this book will define millennials as those born between 1981 and 1996. There will be the caveat, though, that recognizes many of those in this date range do not identify with the label millennial. Additionally, this date range has been chosen specifically due to the types of technology which grew alongside them. Technology will play a crucial role in how museums and cultural institutions market to millennials, therefore it is vital that the age group discussed has similar experiences and technological backgrounds to make the recommendations in this work effective.

In summation, this is what we know for certain. Millennials grew up alongside the rise of technology in the new millennium and see technology as valuable, integral parts of their lives. Studies show more than 75 percent of millennials are active on social media with some sort of profile.[13] Facebook and Instagram appear to be favorites, though many are also active on sites like LinkedIn, Twitter, Pinterest, and Snapchat. Many reportedly see technology as the primary vehicle through which they can live their best lives, which is evident in the rise of the recent trend of branding oneself through social media and technology. This dependence on technology is very important when defining millennials, but they also possess other qualities which are vital to properly identifying the generation.

These are the main qualities of millennials that should be understood when creating programming to engage this patron generation. Millennials:

- Do not want to be labeled
- Are open to change
- Value diversity and inclusion
- Come from varied families, many non-traditional
- Want to make the world a better place
- Incorporate technology into daily life
- Have a heart for charitable causes
- Are well-educated
- Value experiences more than "things"

Millennials are a diverse demographic. It is vital to note here that, like in discussing any generation, we can make generalizations about who they are and what they value, but not all millennials will fall into those analyses. However, in the hopes of reaching a majority of the millennial audience, museum professionals can rely on the available data sets which highlight the

aforementioned characteristics as defining aspects of the millennial generation. These qualities will provide the basis from which programming can be
created to reach them, engage them, and keep them coming back to your
facility time and again.

LITERATURE OVERVIEW: REACHING MILLENNIALS

Reaching millennials, in a general sense, has been a topic saturated with
interest across disciplines for a number of years. Marketing professionals
have attempted to place millennials in categories by creating subgroups more
responsive to targeted marketing. This is a concept that has been applied to
millennials since the members of the generation were preteens. In *Chasing
Youth Culture and Getting It Right*, author Tina Wells gets inside the minds of
millennials as they were living their preteen, teenage, and young adult years.
Wells argues that in order to market to a generation like millennials, who are
often considered unique due to their technological knowledge base, companies need to spend their time understanding subgroups which existed among
millennials as children and young adults and target them accordingly. This
means dividing them based on their personalities and the ways they think,
something she terms "tribes." Wells offers four tribal types for millennials:
techies, preppies, alternatives, and independents.[14] She posits that knowing
each tribe will allow businesses to determine not only who they are marketing to, but also which group would respond best to the product or experience.
For instance, a techie would be the best group to market an advanced Apple
product to, while a preppie would likely be most interested in a mainstream
and popular device. This type of target marketing allows businesses to stop
wasting their efforts chasing a part of a demographic that is not predisposed
to liking or purchasing their product. It means less waste and more profit.
Wells understands one of the basic tenants this book is attempting to promote:
millennials are diverse and like for the products and events which fulfill their
lives to be equally varied. To maintain this audience, museums need to adapt
their advertising efforts to this fact.

Wells published her work in 2011, and while her arguments continue to
hold, there has been much more research done since then. That same year,
Morley Winograd and Michael D. Hais published *Millennial Momentum*, a
work which focused on understanding how millennials were making changes
to the socioeconomic and political landscapes in America.[15] While their

focus is generally on millennials as decision makers in areas like the political process and global interactions, many of their arguments are relevant to museums. Museum professionals might ask themselves why it is so important to understand the political leanings of millennials discussed in this work. The answer is simple. Millennials carry their sense of altruism, commitment to service, and loyalty to philanthropic entities everywhere they go. For some, the government or facets of it are these philanthropic entities; therefore, the ways in which millennials interact with politics can shed light on the ways they might interact with nonprofits committed to the similar ideals of giving voices to the voiceless. While many millennials are grouped in with protestors for causes such as the "Black Lives Matter" and "Me Too" movements, they can also be found in the lower rungs of government working their way toward the senior leadership positions. Millennial representation in government is in no way proportional at this time, but the generation is making a conscious effort to become more actively involved in school boards and other areas of local government, as well as in Congress. This is something museum professionals should pay close attention to; millennials are literally paving the way for the laws of tomorrow, and with it, opportunities for funding.

Not surprisingly, the political awareness of millennials directly correlates to their affinity for diversity and their commitment to seeing that diversity become reality in all facets of life. As early as 2000, when millennials as a generation were first thought to be coming of age, scholars were marking this celebration of diversity as a hallmark of the generation. In *Millennials Rising: The Next Great Generation*, authors Neil Howe and William Strauss gave predictions about the upcoming generation, including that "millennials feel more of an urge to homogenize, to celebrate the ties that bind rather than differences that splinter."[16] They allude to the millennial desire to see diversity as an asset and as a path to inclusion. These two gentlemen are best known for coining the term "millennial" as a way to describe this new, technologically driven generation.[17] As evidenced by numerous studies and research, their prediction that millennials seek inclusion rather than highlighting differences has become truth. Millennials live this truth daily in their spending habits by:

- Purchasing cause-based products more often than others of similar price and value
- Supporting businesses run by disenfranchised groups

- Buying in to the global economy and purchasing products created around the world

They grew up in a world where everyone was told they were special and could make a difference, and in their lives, they take this notion quite literally and seek out opportunities to fulfill those needs. They live and breathe the mantra "We can make a difference."[18] They believe this so profoundly because they were never told otherwise. A love of the global economy, and an almost paradoxical love of local small businesses as well, are also trademarks of millennials and their version of diversity. Millennials are demonstrably more accepting of races, religions, sexual orientation, and other areas than their generational predecessors. This attribute makes millennials more drawn to products, places, and experiences which hold similar values. What this can mean for museums is millennials may respond well to exhibits promoting other cultures or lifestyles, they may buy the locally made products in the gift shops, and they are likely to find fulfillment in paying the price of admission to a facility that gives a portion of its proceeds back to the community or collects donations for clean water systems in underdeveloped nations. Millennials take notice of those businesses and institutions which strive to make a difference, rather than turn a profit. Howe and Strauss all but predicted the effects this adherence to diversity-driven ideals would have on the generation.

WHY INVEST IN MILLENNIALS?

One key question museum professionals may ask themselves is if making the investment in time and funds to attract millennials is really worth the effort. The short answer is yes. Millennials are the largest population group at this point in history and they are also the largest museum patron group, though they are often underserved and therefore not as loyal to those facilities as they could be. This is important to note when deciding on budgets. This book is geared toward small museums, and it is no secret budgets for these facilities are usually quite limited. After all, why spend precious funds on trying to reach and engage them if it is true that the majority of millennials live at home with Mom and Dad, and therefore are unable to spend money they presumably do not have on things like museums? Many millennials may have limited funds and live at home, but that does not stop them from spending those funds on things that really matter to them—things, experiences rather, that are relevant to and have an impact on their lives. They seek out experiences that provide good value for the cost. For instance, the neighborhood coffee shop is integral to the millennial existence because it provides a place for community, free wireless internet access, and the experience of being engaged with the world around them. Museum professionals need to find ways to help their museums become just as impactful by placing its facility's programming within the millennial price range.

Although there are millennials without "real jobs" who have disposable income, let's imagine the possibility of engaging those coveted millennials who do have steady streams of income. The Pew Research Center created a series of studies surrounding millennials to discover how they affect the economy and how they are made up demographically. One of the most surprising findings, and one which is very relevant to this work, is that there are millennials with careers and steady streams of income. As baby boomers begin to cycle out of the patron pool, it is vital that museum professionals start courting the next generation they will rely on for visitation, memberships, volunteer labor, and donations.

Industry professional Colleen Dilenschneider provides invaluable insight into what makes millennials ripe for pursuing relationships with museums. Dilenschneider runs the website *Know Your Own Bone* wherein she posts about a variety of topics related to audience engagement and cultural institutions. Her expertise lies in analyzing data to help "executive decision-makers who are responsible for ensuring the long-term relevance and financial success of their mission-driven organizations."[19] Many of her articles deal directly with millennials and discuss how museums and cultural organizations can reach them and why it is necessary to do so. Dilenschneider provides some of the most recently published insight into how millennials' minds work and how they currently interact with museums and cultural organizations. Some of her most interesting discussions surround concepts including what millennials value in a museum experience, how they might fit into positions on boards for nonprofits, and what subgroups of millennials are actually interested in museums. She argues that millennials are actually a very loyal audience and they want to be involved in museums and cultural organizations, but many millennials hold back from doing so for reasons like poor accessibility or lack of effective communication methods. These facts presented by Dilenschneider and supported by other surveys and data sets are instrumental, real-time resources for museum professionals looking to better understand the future of museums and how millennials can fit into that future.

TYPES OF MILLENNIAL AUDIENCES

Museum leaders can determine four primary subgroups present among millennials: those in co-living situations with limited income, those living independently with steady income, single individuals with children, and people in committed relationships with children. This work will discuss ways to market to all of these subgroups in subsequent chapters. An additional subgroup which should be considered is the childless millennial, either single or in a relationship. These individuals make up another significant percentage of millennials to whom museums and cultural institutions should be marketing. Millennials without children are not necessarily opposed to having them, but generally feel they need to wait until the economy or their current employment situation improves.[20] Products of the recession and witnesses to its toll on their parents' finances, millennials are generally apprehensive to commit to significant life changes for fear of repeating the difficulties of their childhoods.[21] The majority of millennials are renters, not homeowners, partly because renting requires limited commitment but also because living in and around cities can fulfill those needs for ongoing experiences and community.[22] It is noteworthy to recognize that while millennials were taught failure was not an option, they did not completely discount the possibility of failure. This psychological predisposition makes millennials press pause before fully committing to something, for fear of doing the unthinkable and actually failing. Museum professionals can rest assured, though, that most millennials become almost overly committed to a cause or company once they can determine it is worthy of their trust.

Interestingly, studies find this commitment phobia does not always extend to the workforce. Many millennials value the culture of their workplace and the opportunities for personal fulfillment more than pay in some cases.[23] Millennials crave the experience of an innovative and community-like workplace wherein they can grow personally and professionally.[24] There is an argument for applying this same logic to volunteer programs. If millennials are desiring work that is personally fulfilling and has a community impact, there is no need to look further than volunteerism. Studies support this notion, finding that millennials liken volunteerism to charity, a virtue most millennials were taught to value as children and have carried with them into adulthood.[25] It is also helpful that volunteer opportunities allow millennials to build up their resumes, since many entry-level positions require years of experience they likely have to obtain through volunteer opportunities and internships. Many of the millennials in this subgroup of childless individuals fall into this category of those who value volunteerism and actively engage in those opportunities, whether for personal or professional growth, and it is likely a portion of these individuals could become long-term volunteers provided that avenues for growth continued to be present. Millennials can turn their propensity toward self-interest into self-less volunteerism if museums present those volunteer opportunities as something for which millennial contributions are vital.[26]

Millennials want to be needed, which is one instance wherein the sense of narcissism is valid, and they need to feel invaluable in the workplace or as volunteers in order to become committed.[27] Think of courting millennials to be volunteers as a similar process to how a hiring manager would court new, groundbreaking talent in the workplace. That manager would take the time to highlight all of the aspects of the potential employee which make him or her vital to the operations and growth of the facility. Millennials do not want to be another workhorse; each one wants to feel like a rare find for the facility. Museum professionals can capitalize on this need to be vital to the community by seeking out these millennials and offering them the impactful experiences they crave as volunteers at their facilities.

Another vital subgroup is the millennial parent. Despite the fact millennials are waiting to have children at a later age, there are still large numbers of parents and single working mothers within the age group. In fact, as of 2017, it was noted by the Pew Research Center that millennials were becoming parents at the rate of over one million new moms each year.[28] Upon first glance, this may not appear very relevant. However, a closer look is needed here. It is increasingly evident from various studies that millennials value atypical education and learning styles, opting for more hands-on experiential learning programs. Millennial parents, or "parennials" as they have been recently termed, often make the same choices regarding their child's education. When given the choice between public school, which studies show millennials are losing faith in as part of an overall feeling of the country being in freefall,[29] and alternative forms of education for their children, many opt for the alternative. This comes in forms such as parochial schools, co-ops, gifted programs, and homeschooling. These millennial parents, many of whom are likely single mothers,[30] are a ripe target for marketing educational programming at museums. Mothers crave experiences for their children just as much as they crave those experiences for themselves. Museum leaders should be paying attention to this trend and capitalizing on it.

HOW THIS BOOK WILL HELP YOU REACH THEM

Taking all of this information into account—who millennials are, why they are important, what makes them relevant to museums—this book will guide you through the difficult task of assessing how you are currently reaching and engaging this age group and suggest ways in which current strategies can be updated. This book will ask you to reexamine your preconceived notions about millennials and adapt your museum programming to better reach this audience. The focus throughout will be on programming—creating it, implementing it, and making it successful enough to offer again. Millennials are experiential learners and crave experiences over products; therefore, museum leaders need to focus on crafting community for millennials through museum experiences. You will be asked to reassess how your current programming for millennials, if you have any in place, scores in certain categories. In short, your museum staff will need to check the museum's A.U.R.A. to determine if changes can be made to elevate your millennial-based programming. You will evaluate your programs in the fields of accessibility, uniqueness, relevance, and approachability, each one chapter at a time. You will be asked to reflect on each concept. Is my museum accessible, physically and financially, to millennials? Is the programming offered at my museum unique in concept or to my facility, and not too commercial? Is the programming we offer relevant to millennial interests as well as the mission of the facility? Is my museum inclusive and inviting to all millennials, and lacking an intimidation factor? Answers to these questions and others like it will provide valuable insight into the areas in which your museum can make improvements to its programming. If you are starting from scratch, this work will guide you on the path to creating programming geared toward millennials. Each chapter will provide examples of actual programs in use at various museums, as well as suggestions for future programs, which could be adapted and implemented at other museums. References will also be made to programs which have not worked well, with explanations as to why this was the case. By the end of this book, your museum should feel equipped to try new and innovative programs, or even expand old or current programs, to meet the needs of the most relevant consumer group of this century.

It is vital museums discover how to tap into this generation as volunteers, members, and donors through the gateway of museum programming. After all, the future of museums really rests in the hands of the millennials.

Let's get started.

NOTES

1. Joel Stein, "Millennials: The Me Me Me Generation," http://time.com/247/millennials-the-me-me-me-generation/, last modified May 20, 2013 (accessed April 15, 2018).

2. "State of the American Workplace," Gallup, 2013, http://employeeengagement.com/wpcontent/uploads/2013/06/Gallup-2013-State-of-the-American-Workplace-Report.pdf (accessed December 18, 2017).

3. "Marketing to Millennials," *The Hartman Group*, 2010, http://www.hartman-group.com/hartbeat/marketing-to-millennials.

4. Michael Dimock, "Defining Generations: Where Millennials End and Post-Millennials Begin," Pew Research Center, Washington, D.C. (March 1, 2018), accessed March 10, 2018, http://www.pewresearch.org/fact-tank/2018/03/01/defining-generations-where-millennials-end-and-post-millennials-begin/.

5. "Millennials: Confident. Connected. Open to Change," Pew Research Center, Washington, D.C. (February 24, 2010), accessed December 8, 2017, http://www.pewsocialtrends.org/2010/02/24/millennials-confident-connected-open-to-change/.

6. There are hundreds of books and articles which suggest millennial birthdate ranges. The 1977 start date is taken from *The Millennials: Americans Born 1977–1994* (2009) by the New Strategist Editors. The 2003 end date is taken from *Millennial Momentum: How a New Generation Is Remaking America* (2011) by Morley Winograd and Michael D. Hais. The most accepted date range until the 2018 Pew Research determination of 1981–1996 was 1982–2000, which was purported by Neil Howe and William Strauss in *Millennials Rising: The Next Great Generation* (2000).

7. "Most Millennials Resist the 'Millennial' Label," Pew Research Center, Washington, D.C. (September 3, 2015), accessed January 3, 2018, http://www.people-press.org/2015/09/03/most-millennials-resist-the-millennial-label/.

8. Pew Research Center, "Most Millennials Resist the 'Millennial' Label."

9. Bruce Drake, "6 New Findings about Millennials," Pew Research Center, Washington, D.C. (March 7, 2014), accessed January 3, 2018, http://www.pewresearch.org/fact-tank/2014/03/07/6-new-findings-about-millennials/.

10. Pew Research Center, "Millennials: Confident. Connected. Open to Change."

11. Drake, "6 New Findings about Millennials."

12. Richard Fry, "5 facts about Millennial Households," Pew Research Center, Washington, D.C. (September 6, 2017), accessed December 8, 2017, http://www.pewresearch.org/fact-tank/2017/09/06/5-facts-about-millennial-households/.

13. Pew Research Center, "Millennials: Confident. Connected. Open to Change."

14. Wells, *Chasing Youth Culture and Getting It Right*, 48–49.

15. Morley Winograd and Michael D. Hais, *Millennial Momentum: How a New Generation Is Remaking America* (New Brunswick, NJ: Rutgers University Press, 2011).

16. Neil Howe and William Strauss, *Millennials Rising: The Next Great Generation* (New York: Vintage Books, 2000), 221.

17. Howe and Strauss, *Millennials Rising*, 6.

18. Tania Bucic, Jennifer Harris, and Denni Arli. "Ethical Consumers Among the Millennials: A Cross-National Study." *Journal of Business Ethics* 110, No. 1 (September 2012): 115, http://www.jstor.org/stable/41684017.

19. Colleen Dilenschneider, "Colleen Dilenschneider—Data-Informed Resource for Cultural Executives," *Know Your Own Bone* (blog), https://www.colleendilen.com/ (accessed January 10, 2018).

20. Drake, "6 New Findings about Millennials."

21. Jeff Fromm and Marissa Vidler, *Millennials with Kids: Marketing to this Powerful and Surprisingly Different Generation of Parents* (New York: AMACOM 2015), 9.

22. Fry, "5 Facts about Millennial Households."

23. Eddy S. W. Ng, Linda Schweitzer, and Sean T. Lyons, "New Generation, Great Expectations," *Journal of Business and Psychology* 25, No. 2, Special Issue: "Millennials and the World of Work: What You Didn't Know You Didn't Know" (June 2010): 282, http://www.jstor.org/stable/40605786.

24. Ng, Schweitzer, and Lyons, "New Generation, Great Expectations," 283.

25. Jay Price, "Getting Ready for the Next Generation," American Association for State and Local History. *History News* 60, No. 2 (Spring 2005): 19, http://www.jstor.org/stable/42654012.

26. Jeanine S. Stewart, Elizabeth Goad Oliver, Karen S. Cravens, and Shigehiro Oishi, "Managing Millennials: Embracing Generational Differences," *Business Horizons* 60 (2017): 50, http://dx.doi.org/10.1016/j.bushor.2016.08.011.

27. Keith R. Credo, Patricia A. Lanier, Curtis F. Matherine III, and Susie S. Cox, "Narcissism and Entitlement in Millennials: The Mediating Influence of Community

Service Self Efficacy on Engagement," *Personal and Individual Differences* 101 (2016): 193, http://dx.doi.org/10.1016/j.paid.2016.05.370.

28. Gretchen Livingston, "More Than a Million Millennials are Becoming Moms Each Year," Pew Research Center, Washington, D.C. (January 3, 2017), accessed February 21, 2018, http://www.pewresearch.org/fact-tank/2017/01/03/more-than-a -million-millennials-are-becoming-moms-each-year/.

29. Samantha Smith, "Patriotic, Honest and Selfish: How Americans Describe . . . Americans," Pew Research Center, Washington, D.C. (December 11, 2015), accessed December 21, 2017, http://www.pewresearch.org/fact-tank/2015/12/11/patriotic -honest-and-selfish-how-americans-describe-americans/.

30. Fry, "5 facts about Millennial Households."

2

A: "Affordability"

ONE of the hot topics in the museum world is the question of whether charging admission, be it to museums themselves or to specific events and programs, helps or hinders visitation to those sites. Such a discussion extends beyond general admission into planning special exhibits, programs, and festivals. This chapter seeks to provide insight into the varieties of millennial budgets, the spending habits of millennials, how millennials view the relationship between value and cost, and how museum leaders can create affordable programming with limited funds.

By the end of this chapter, you should be able to identify what the data sets reveal about millennial incomes, how and why millennials choose to spend their money, and what museum professionals can do to make their facilities worthy of the cost of admission. This chapter will examine how subsets of millennials determine affordability and value. We will also discuss how museum professionals can make these programs affordable for their facilities, as well as their patrons. Specific examples will be included to provide insight into programs that have worked to generate a loyal, interactive millennial audience.

MILLENNIAL INCOME: WHAT THE DATA REVEALS

Unsurprisingly, much of the available data sets support the assumption that millennials live at home with their parents, or at least with roommates.[1] Many of these individuals are held back from purchasing their own homes due to the overwhelming costs of student loans and medical bills. With the rising cost and the everchanging, hotly debated structure of the country's healthcare system, millennials are sometimes forced to choose between paying healthcare premiums and paying their rent. Unlike the thirty-year period after World War II when a young person could start and work his or her way up in a job complete with a livable salary, retirement funds, and company-supported healthcare, today's young adults are finding it increasingly improbable to locate full-time work, let alone positions with the aforementioned benefits included.

The solution, for many, has been to work multiple part-time positions to make ends meet. This is often referred to in colloquial terms as the "gig economy." There really is no single definition for this trend, but it generally means a person takes on a single project in exchange for monetary compensation and without the promise of future work or job security. These positions are unlikely to provide access to benefits like healthcare, paid or sick leave, or retirement. The Bureau of Labor Statistics admits one of the issues with this type of economy is it is difficult to track on paper.[2] When one person works multiple contract jobs alongside other part-time work, gathering statistics on those positions is very hard for statisticians. This is one of the primary reasons why understanding the millennial generation is so difficult: museum professionals have very limited access to real-time data.

This gig economy situation provides little room for millennials to grow, let alone meet their basic needs. As a result, when a medical emergency occurs and a millennial is without healthcare or sick leave, termination or a spiral toward poverty is often inevitable. These types of circumstances eventually lead many millennials to live at home with their parents, not the creatively crafted narrative of entitlement so often attributed to this segment of society. Most millennials do not want to live at home any more than they want to go without healthcare. Most still believe in the American Dream, but many feel America has given up on them.

Millennials, as a whole, do earn less money than their parents did at a comparable age. This is, in part, because of economic fluctuations and downturns, but also due to the role and necessity of education in a millennial's life. Formal college education has become a baseline for potential employers and a hallmark of a reliable and prepared workforce. In order for millennials to qualify for full-time, and many times part-time, work in their fields, they are expected to have at minimum a four-year degree. Most employers expect work beyond that point including master's, doctoral, and postdoctoral experience and degrees. Unfortunately, according to a study done by the Urban Institute, the cost of master's degrees between 1996 and 2016 has grown nearly 79 percent, and that number just includes tuition and fees, not considering the cost of room and board.[3] *Forbes* also reported a doubling of college debt for students graduating in 2003 versus 2016. The 2003 graduate left with approximately $18,000, while the 2016 graduate left with over $37,000.[4] With the expectations for education set so high, millennials without means are often forced to take on high-dollar loans to afford the education considered prerequisite for employment.

The nature and availability of these loans has changed over the last few decades, along with the cost of a college education. At this point in time, the median loan balance for a bachelor's degree is in the tens of thousands of dollars. Graduate program work can take this number into the hundreds of thousands of dollars. When millennials graduate and enter the marketplace, they often find little return on their investment. Most employers do not aid in the repayment of student loans, and while the government does offer assistance for those who qualify, the assistance itself is often inadequate. In many ways, it can feel like the education system has set them up to fail.

There are millennials who do not experience the burden of student loans. Such individuals likely hailed from affluent families who subsidized their college experience or attended low-cost community or technical colleges as a stepping-stone toward employment. Many of these individuals could not afford the cost of education even with loans, and therefore there is a large segment of the millennial population that did not receive a college education at all. Even in terms of education and income, millennials are not able to be labeled.

According to an article by Michael Hobbes, millennials are in much more dire straits than purported. Hobbes discusses the financial health, or rather lack thereof, of the millennial generation. He offers a variety of graphics based on data from the College Board, National Center for Education Statistics, and the Institute for Policy Studies, among others.[5] His conclusions are eye-opening, yet expected. Hobbes purports that millennials are putting off making big purchases and life changes due to their debts, a conclusion also supported by the Bureau of Labor Statistics, which reported a ratio of 1:3 millennial homeowners versus millennial renters.[6] Additionally, millennials have

FIGURE 2.1
Student Debt versus Opportunities
Created for Publication by Morven Moeller, 2018

to work fifteen times as many hours as the baby boomers did to pay for four years of a college education, which the same Bureau of Labor Statistics study reports 72 percent of millennials have.[7] And as icing on the cake, millennials who graduated just after the recession are making almost $30,000 less yearly than their pre-recession counterparts.[8] Hobbes points toward an inevitable conclusion: millennials are simply not set up for financial success.

This does not mean that millennials have given up on the idea of having a fulfilling, productive life. Many find creative ways to budget their funds to pave the way for happiness in their daily lives despite the low digits in their bank accounts. The cloud of financial doom that continues to hover over millennials is parted only by positive, enriching life experiences and the hope of making a difference. We cannot forget the studies cited in the previous chapter, which tell the story that millennials want to make a difference and feel they can do so. This sense of positivity does carry into their daily lives, regardless of the financial circumstances they often suffer. This mindset points them toward viewing museum attendance and other recreational activities as forms of escapism, and desperately needed ones at that.

The economic circumstances of millennials do contribute to their ability to patronize certain facilities. Most live in the present and few feel they can save for the future. This makes a difference when examining how millennials budget. There are fewer millennials, and adults in general, actively including retirement or emergency savings in their monthly budgets.[9] Many use whatever funds they have left over to create experiences for themselves that contribute to their quality of life or allow them to escape the perils and responsibilities of life. This is the millennial priority. When thinking about priorities and the millennial budget, there are a few takeaway points museum staff should remember:

- For most millennials, money is scarce due to a poor job market, rising debt, lack of job stability, and absence of work-related benefits like healthcare and retirement
- Millennials have limited funds and associate dollars with value
- Millennials are more willing to use any extra funds they possess to have experiences, rather than buy products
- Millennials expect the money they spend to contribute to their quality of life and like their entertainment venues to provide a form of escapism

VALUE, COST, AND MILLENNIAL SPENDING HABITS

Keeping all of the statistics in mind, it should be obvious that most millennials do not have deep pockets or large disposable incomes. This does not mean millennials avoid leisurely activities or do not contribute to the market economy. In fact, millennials are on their way to becoming the largest and most vital contributors to economic success. According to an article from Forbes, "Millennials are quickly becoming the most important consumers encountered by most types of business, with a spending power that is estimated to be worth $10 trillion over their lifetimes."[10] As baby boomers enter retirement and generation Xers move toward it, millennials are coming to the forefront as valued consumers. As evidenced in the previous section, times are hard for millennials. Still, they make purchases and spend their funds where and when they can. Millennial values and ideas about quality of life make the greatest contribution to their spending decisions in terms of nonessential purchases. Museums, like many other forms of entertainment and leisure, fall into this category.

Studies show most millennials are concerned about money and their financial futures. They appear, however, to place a higher value on having enriching experiences over saving for "ideas" that feel out of reach or intangible, such as retirement. Having grown up with economic uncertainty and many now in the throes of financial crisis, they seek refuge in having meaningful experiences in their everyday lives. Millennials associate dollars with value; they want their purchases to have meaning in their lives and often in the lives of others. This focus on experience and value serves as the undercurrent through which millennials make their purchasing decisions.

Social media plays a vital role in determining how millennials view the value of a facility, and subsequently, whether or not they will patronize those institutions. Millennials have an expectation that brands that are worthy of their time and money will be available at their fingertips. Author Tina Wells has described this expectation best, stating millennials "need instant results, instant action, and instant gratification."[11] An active social media presence allows for that connection and contributes to the millennial's perceived sense of value toward the facility. These same brands are also expected to actively engage in relationship building with millennials by making them a part of the conversation, many times even involving them in the creation of the brand identity itself. These millennials can then become Brand Ambassadors, or people who actively help your facility market itself on social media or otherwise because they feel the facility is valuable.[12] Millennials crave experiences, even in the way they receive marketing campaigns. In fact, they want to be involved in the creation of those campaigns and help mold them to fit their needs,[13] therefore making the facility valuable in their eyes. The most successful museums and cultural institutions actively involve their millennial social media base in the creation of their programs and solicit feedback from that audience frequently. Millennials are loyal to these types of facilities because these facilities place value on their input. In essence, millennials perceive value in places which value them. In order for cultural institutions to translate as valuable, they must insist on collaboration with a millennial audience through the places where they can always be found: social media platforms.

Textbox 2.1

CREATING VALUE WITH SOCIAL MEDIA

Millennials use social media platforms as an indicator of perceived value. It is your institution's job to make sure millennials can easily discern what your museum brings to the table. To accomplish this, start by examining your social media identity. Do all of your platforms give out the same message? Have you streamlined descriptions, logos, and branding? If yes, you have completed step one. Step two is to get the attention of millennials and keep it. To do this, make sure your facility posts regularly, preferably once daily on all platforms, and that all posts are relevant and specific to your museum. Pictures are always a plus. Use hashtags when they are applicable. Lastly, make your social media platforms participatory. Create polls, ask questions, and provide areas for visitors to post their own photos and experiences at your facility. Take the time to follow up with those interactions. Creating such dialogue will build brand loyalty, continually engage your audience, and help millennials place value on your facility.

MILLENNIAL VIEWS ON "THE COST OF ADMISSION"

When I engage with other museum professionals in discussion over price points that will attract a millennial audience to a program or event, the first answer to the question of what to charge is often "nothing." Up until I began researching for this book, I will admit, I was also of the mindset that millennials want and need programs to be as close to free as possible, with the cost preferably being always free. My research, though, has convinced me that millennials are not always solely on the lookout for free programs. Since they often associate cost with value, wouldn't it make sense that if things are free all of the time, they might lose their perceived value? I believe this thought occurs in the minds of many millennials and, as a result, many are willing to pay the price of admission for programs that speak value to them.

This concept is supported by industry leader Colleen Dilenschneider, who asserts that free and discounted admission often results in lower visitor satisfaction.[14] Additionally, she states that while there might be an initial bump in visitation, it is not usually by first-time visitors, but by those already interested in your facility.[15] The long-term effects of these free and discounted days are not as positive as museum leaders think. Dilenschneider states, "Data suggest that discounting negatively influences the *very two factors* that drive visitation in the long-term: Satisfaction and reputation."[16] While her findings are not about millennials specifically, because we now know millennials are the most populous group visiting museums, we can determine many in this demographic are part of the findings in this data. What this means for museum professionals is we need to stop thinking millennials and other visitors will only attend if programming is free; instead, we need to focus on providing a valuable experience in exchange for admission.

In an interview with fellow millennial Raven Hudson, I inquired as to how she felt about paying for admission to a museum. Her answer fell in line with how I believe millennials perceive value. She admitted that, like many millennials, her first thought is often to find the cheapest thing to do that will provide a fun experience. However, she also stated, "When I know something is free, I know it will always be there so I do not make it a priority." She added that she "will spend money on an experience that is unique" because she knows it might be her "only chance to do this, and it will never happen again."[17] While millennials enjoy facilities with free admission because they are accessible, they are willing to pay for admission for tours and events when they think not attending means missing out on a memorable experience.

Textbox 2.2

"I will spend money on an experience that is unique." —Raven Hudson, 25

Millennials prefer very inexpensive programs but are not opposed to spending money on cultural experiences. One notable example comes from a museum in Norfolk, Virginia, called the Hermitage Museum and Gardens. The Hermitage hosted a museum exhibition of Burning Man art in 2017 and found the experience to be very successful, specifically with a millennial audience. Marketing Manager Jennifer Lucy believes what drew such a large crowd of millennials was the programming focused on inclusivity and community involvement.[18] The exhibition included weekly Thursday evening programming the museum termed Burning Man Nights and featured local artists and musicians, plus an opening and closing reception. The programming created around the exhibition attracted over 7,000 participants. For a small to mid-size museum, this was extremely successful.

The Thursday evening Burning Man Nights program was by far the most fruitful, accounting for over 5,000 of the attendees to the exhibition. Each night varied in its offerings, all of which related to the themes of the art. Sometimes the evening would feature food trucks and an outdoor bar; other times it would focus on community partnerships and performances. These evenings were dynamic, creative, inclusive, and affordable. Yes, the key here is affordable. Admission for each program was $15 for adults and $12 for museum members, students, children ages six to twelve, and active duty military. Children under five were admitted free of charge, which likely persuaded many millennial parents to partake in the exhibition. These attendees were reached through a marketing campaign that was supported by the community through local organizations. Some groups designed images for advertisements and others focused on promoting the event locally and regionally. Social media provided the bulk of the advertising for these events and was supplemented through posters, print ads, and postcards directed toward an artsy audience.[19]

Textbox 2.3

"When I found out we were doing this exhibit, I thought, 'we have to collaborate . . . with everyone in the community . . . that's what Burning Man is all about.'" —Jennifer Lucy, Marketing Manager, Hermitage Museum and Gardens

This artsy audience was readily found in Norfolk's relatively new arts district known as the N.E.O.N.: New Energy of Norfolk. The Hermitage Museum and Gardens created opportunities for partnership with entities involved in this sector. The museum's staff wanted the patrons of the arts district to feel like the programming for the exhibition was made with them in mind, so they made it so. The museum hosted a community forum to ensure the exhibition would be tailor-made for those already predisposed to being interested in Burning Man art.[20] It just so happened that the audience most interested was millennials, and they turned out consistently to ensure the event's success. The moral of this story is that these millennials had a voice that they wanted to be heard and appreciated the collaborative nature of this museum's programming. They were able to take a sense of ownership in the programming and their attendance was an active show of support for the efforts made by their friends and coworkers in the art scene. They helped to design programming that was affordable for them, while also remaining relevant to the Hermitage Museum and Gardens and its mission. This event was a success because it highlighted millennial voices, rather than silencing them. Museum professionals should take notice of this collaborative approach to program design.

Textbox 2.4

Event Highlight: *Burning Man Nights*

Facility: Hermitage Museum and Gardens

Location: Norfolk, Virginia

Budget: >$300,000 (Mid-sized museum)

Staff Size: 9 paid, plus volunteers

Event Description: "Experience The Art of Burning Man at night along with a variety of interactive programs, temporary art installations, live performances, and more. Encounter something different during each Burning Man Night! The grounds and museum will be open all evening and Burning Man Docents will be stationed throughout the exhibition to engage visitors. Guests may purchase a drink from the bar while exploring the site. Gates open at 7. (Pulled directly from http://thehermit agemuseum.org/burning-man-nights/)

Average Attendance: 5,000+ (throughout the exhibition, June–October 2017)

Ways Marketed: Social media platforms, posters, postcards, print ads, local organizations

Marketing Manager's Take: Burning Man "brought out new demographics we didn't have before . . . if we had not had that community forum and really made it the community's show, it would not have been as successful." —Jennifer Lucy, Marketing Manager

Why It Works: This event offered an affordable ticket price of $15 and under, which made it a low-cost opportunity for millennials to experience art in a unique, accessible environment. The development of this programming was very collaborative, including the hosting of a community forum with the local arts scene, many of which were millennials. The evenings were interactive, educational, inclusive, and entertaining. Millennials took advantage of this rare exhibition in full force, many with their children. Staff report an uptick in millennial memberships to the museum because of the frequency and popularity of these nights, which offered discounted admission to members. Millennials were able to participate with the museum in the creation of the programming, which increased their brand loyalty and gave them a sense of ownership of the facility. Involving millennials in the creation of programming is an ideal way to engage them and keep them interested in your facility.

Another example of successful millennial-oriented programming is the Drink Up, Tweet Up event hosted annually by the Campbell House Museum in St. Louis, Missouri. The event is held during an early evening in October and features libations, food, and music all donated by docents, board members, and community partners. The museum accepts monetary donations, but the event itself and all the fixings are free of charge to attendees. The focus is on small-batch homebrews of beer and gin that are created by a local blogger and cosponsor. These libations are served with the museum's mission in mind with each beer that is brewed being themed annually based on a Campbell family member. Music is generally supported financially by a board member and a local restaurant provides the catering. During this time, the museum is also available for tours. The Campbell House Museum does very well with this event, bringing in close to 150 participants each year, most of which are millennials. When asked how he felt this event fit into the museum's mission, Executive Director Andy Hahn commented that part of their mission statement is to enliven the history of the house, which this event certainly does.[21] He seemed to be alluding to the creation of a relaxed, informal atmosphere that allowed people to experience the museum in a new, more lively way.[22] Based on the turnout, I would say they have found a wonderful way to reconcile their mission with millennial interests. In fact, this event serves as the gateway through which these millennials discover and begin a relationship with the museum, and isn't that the entire point?

Textbox 2.5

Event Highlight: Drink Up, Tweet Up

Facility: Campbell House Museum

Location: St. Louis, Missouri

Budget: <$300,000

Staff Size: 2 paid, plus volunteers

Event Description: "Join the Campbell House Museum and Distilled History for an evening of music, food, and potent potables. Explore St. Louis' history through the lens of beer and spirits in and around the walls of one of America's most accurately restored 19th century buildings. Enjoy food donated by Maya Cafe and beer donated by Schlafly and Urban Chestnut. Distilled History's Cameron Collins will be providing homemade gin and Campbell themed beer. This event is completely FREE to the public, but limited to the 21 and over crowd." (Pulled directly from http://www.campbellhousemuseum.org/event/drink-up-tweet-up-2017)

Average Attendance: 150

Ways Marketed: Social media platforms, Distilled History blog (local blogger)

Director's Take: "This event often serves as their first exposure to the museum . . . it feels informal." —Andy Hahn, Executive Director

Why It Works: This event offers an affordable, unique experience with food and drink catered directly to the mission and history of the museum. Additionally, it runs on a fall evening during what the Executive

Director terms a "happy hour" time frame of 5–7 p.m. The event lessens the intimidation factor by offering an informal atmosphere complete with time for socializing in the garden with friends. Best of all, the event costs the museum only its time. The cost of the music is generally covered by a board member, the liquid libations are created and provided by a docent, and the food is also donated. The event is cross-promoted by a local history blogger, Distilled History. What a fantastic way to partner with the volunteer staff and community!

These events do bring up an important question, though: Do museums need to have alcohol-focused events in order to attract millennials? I would argue the answer is no. Yes, millennials are drawn to alcohol, but I do not believe it is the primary reason they attend these events; rather, they attend because the event offers a unique, affordable experience for them. In the case of the Burning Man Nights and the Drink Up, Tweet Up, alcohol was simply an added incentive. The primary draw for the Burning Man Nights program was the art-focused programming. Their innovative use of the local community in creating programming geared toward the arts crowd resulted in crowdsourced ideas for weekly entertainment. This program came in the form of various local artists, eccentrics, and entertainers, all of whom were staples in the local art community. Refreshments were icing on the cake; the entertainment and rarity of the art were the main acts. For the Drink Up, Tweet Up, the "wow" factor came in the form of personalized homebrews created by a docent of the museum. Each year, the brew is specially crafted with a member of the Campbell family in mind. It is this personalization of the beer that attracts millennials, not the beer itself. It is also helpful that the event is promoted and cosponsored by a local blogger, who is known for his knowledge of the liquid libations. In both cases, the rarity of the "product" offered at the event made the event feel special and worth attending. The low and free admission prices gave millennials the extra push to attend the event.

DESIGNING AFFORDABLE PROGRAMMING FOR THE FACILITY

While it is essential to make the cost of admission affordable for a millennial audience, it is equally necessary to make the cost of putting on such programming manageable for the small and mid-size museum budget. There are a variety of tips and tricks to help your facility cut down on costs, many of which you may already be implementing. Still, it is valuable to discuss them more fully here to determine if there are areas wherein your museum staff can improve the facility's funding possibilities and decrease its spending.

One of the most underused sources for cutting down costs is collaboration with local businesses and groups in the community. Many institutions do not actively engage their surrounding business communities, whether it is due to an underlying feeling of negativity toward soliciting aid or simply a lack of knowledge of where to start the process. All museum professionals should be taking advantage of the business and cultural facilities around them. The big bonus is that the millennial audience loves community collaboration and often supports such efforts, as evidenced by the two examples given in this chapter. You can save money and increase your audience by instituting this one change.

The downside to community collaboration is that your facility often re-linquishes some control over the programming; however, the benefits far outweigh this factor. In many cases the community partners add innovative ideas to the programs that may not have been realized previously by the museum's staff during the planning process. To begin locating potential community partners, review your museum's mission and roster of special events. Take the time to examine how each event fits into your mission statement and determine if there are areas in which your programming could improve. For example, perhaps you run a historic house museum with a mission to educate the public about life in the eighteenth century. You consistently offer living history programs that meet this need, but you desire your programming to be more interactive and immersive to appeal to a younger audience. One way you might improve upon this programming would be to find a local craft guild and ask them to cosponsor classes or demonstrations at your facility. This would likely not cost the museum anything, except supplies, which could be shared with the artisans. Or, you could ask the artisans to donate time and supplies in exchange for free advertising on your social media platforms. Many local artists are amenable to exchanging services, especially when they will receive advertising or promotion to a new or expanded audience.

Another example of collaboration would be partnering with a local theater or school arts program to find fresh talent to bring music and performance art into your facility. Many students look for ways to add to their portfolios or to create relationships that might lead to paid work in the future. The

Hunter House Victorian Museum has pulled from local musicians and artists frequently for evening performances and has witnessed a rise in attendance for those events which include music and new talent. The museum has also partnered with other nonprofits and businesses to offer programs it could not offer by itself. Most notably was a recent fashion show held at a local historic church-turned-restaurant within one block of the facility. The restaurant agreed to a set price for the three-course luncheon, and the museum staff priced the tickets at twice the price to accommodate for the cost. The staff wanted the show to feature fashions throughout the nineteenth century and recruited models from the Victorian Society in America, Regency Society of Virginia, and museum docents and friends. They even advertised on Facebook for models from the community and discovered a half dozen people with appropriate outfits, many of which were made by the models themselves. Over half of the models were millennials, who were happy to have an excuse to dress up and show off their handiwork. The event would not have been possible without the willingness of the restaurant to host the event because the museum was too small to accommodate the number of attendees. The nonprofit and community assistance with models and costumes was invaluable.

In addition to community partnerships with the content of special programs, it is always ideal to ask for donations for refreshments for local

---

Textbox 2.6

QUICK TIP: MAKE EVENTS AFFORDABLE FOR YOU

Millennial budgets are small, and many times, so are museum budgets. Struggling to afford offering new programming? Consider your local community assets. What organizations, small businesses, or institutions are in your vicinity that may be able to help? Community partnerships may play key roles in your success. Do not be afraid to solicit donations. Ask the local theater to provide actors or costumes for an immersive program. See if a local bakery will donate refreshments in return for marketing their business. Collaborate and offer joint programming such as fashion shows, lectures, festivals, silent auctions, or other events. Museums are community staples; the community is often happy to help.

museums. If you have local breweries, wineries, or bakeries near you, take advantage of them. Offer them a tax write-off in exchange for goods. Find food trucks or small catering companies and ask them to set up at your programs and festivals. Host silent auctions and ask for donations from local small businesses who are eager to promote their business to a new audience for minimal cost. Hold a themed bake sale at your facility, and ask other nonprofits who are relevant to your mission to donate sweets. When able, always try to trade free advertising for goods and services. Social media is a free service and offering to post about the entity supporting your facility is a cost-free way to repay their generosity.

PRACTICAL APPLICATIONS

In summation, millennial pocketbooks are limited, but not empty. They equate cost with value and crave experiences over products. The way to reach a millennial audience is to offer affordable programming that aligns with millennial values and adds to their quality of life. This looks different for each subgroup of millennials: the single, childless millennial, the millennial in a committed relationship, and the millennial parent. Let's take a look at each and determine what is "affordable" for each group.

The single, childless millennial is, perhaps, one of the easiest groups to market programming to because they are the primary decision maker in their lives. These individuals are interested in having experiences that are valuable to them, either alone or in groups. They experience more freedom of choice when deciding how to spend their money and time. This is reflected in the type of programming that may appeal to them. Members of this subgroup may be interested in programming that is reflective, educational, or provides opportunities for engagement with others with similar interests.

Museum professionals will find a willing audience in this subgroup and can expand their interests by offering low and no-cost programs to get them in the door. Millennials in relationships also seek valuable experiences; the difference is that they often have another decision maker in the mix. Partners with similar interests will be easiest to market to, while those relationships reflective of the "opposites attract" philosophy might prove troublesome. Museum professionals should take note of the likelihood that those interested in their events may have uninterested partners.

This is when reflecting on the variety of programming offered by one facility is imperative. To illustrate, we have a millennial audience that is just as diverse as the human population as a whole at the Hunter House Victorian Museum, where I currently serve as Museum Director. Those millennials who attend our afternoon teas are not usually the same individuals who attend our open houses or scavenger hunts. Millennial audiences are diverse and require a variety of programming. For example, a husband and wife might attend our date night lecture series because it is a date night for them; however, I might see the husband at a future event cohosted with the Tidewater Coin Club and the wife at our 19th Century Fashion Show. I do not expect that they will always attend together; therefore, it is vital that our programming focuses on marketing to them as individuals while keeping in mind the necessity of offering opportunities for them to come together at another time. This is how we have been successful in maintaining a millennial audience: diversifying our programming. For examples, please see table 2.1.

Millennial parents are another demographic entirely. Like millennials in relationships, millennial parents often come to the table with two voices: that of themselves and that of their children. It is important for museum professionals to appeal to both interests. When attempting to attract parents, value is key. Most millennial parents who regularly take their children to museums do so because they see museums as educational facilities that are affordable. They trust museums. They see them as valuable. For parents, affordable can mean many things. For most, there is a focus on time—time as money, time as valuable, time as limited. Authors Jeff Fromm and Marissa Vidler are absolutely on track with the millennial parent mindset when they state a "higher value placed on time means that new moms are more interested in creating experiences for their children and families that are worthwhile and a good use of their time."[23] This unquestionably plays into the decision-making process. With so many options saturating the market for children's time, museums have to ensure family-friendly programming is competitive in cost and value. Free and low-cost programs are crucial to attracting and maintaining a millennial parent audience. For examples, please see table 2.2.

Taking all of this information into account, museum professionals should feel equipped with the necessary knowledge to determine how to make programming affordable for millennials. This does not always have to look like

Table 2.1. Free and Low-Cost Event Options for Adults

Event	Proposed Cost of Admission	Cost to Museum	Tips
Lectures/Topic-Driven Roundtables	Up to $10	Potentially Free	• Pick topics unique to your facility • Use speakers who do not require fees (staff, volunteers, community members) • Ask for donations for refreshments
Music in the Garden	Up to $10	Potentially Free	• Host the event on an evening in the spring or fall, when the weather is manageable • Try to find local musicians, either students or professionals, who will have no cost or low-cost fees • Ask for donations for refreshments
Art or Fashion Showcase	Up to $20	Potentially Free	• Partner with local colleges • Find local artists with relevant work to display • Have a Meet and Greet with the artist or the models/designers • Ask for donations for refreshments
Open House	Free	Potentially Free	• Invite guests to a day of music and refreshments at your facility • Have both music and refreshments donated • Offer a raffle for tickets to come back for a tour, or for a free membership to the facility • Be sure to include some evening hours to accommodate the working crowd
Scavenger Hunt	Free	Potentially Free	• Collaborate with local colleges and libraries to create materials • Offer refreshments, preferably donated, at the finish line • Make the stops on the hunt relevant to your museum and its mission • Include a social media component within the hunt to encourage promotion of your facility

Table 2.2. Free and Low-Cost Event Options for Children

Event	Proposed Cost of Admission	Cost to Museum	Tips
Storytime	Free	Potentially Free	• Offer weekend options with the working parent in mind—this may also cut down on the competition • Be mindful of common naptimes when scheduling • Choose stories that are relevant to the content and mission of your museum • Advertise with local parent groups, through the community boards and recreation centers, and through social media • When able, find a fun character to do the readings • Offer sensible snacks, preferably donated
Crafts	Up to $5	Potentially Free	• With so many museums and libraries offering these types of programs, it is essential for your museum to find a project that is unique • Ask local businesses or volunteers and board members for donations for materials • Collaborate with outreach organizations for ideas, helping hands, and even materials
Outdoor Play	Up to $5	Potentially Free	• If you have a garden, consider hosting a field day or time of exploration for the little ones • Gear each event toward your mission and relate the activities to an educational component • Have sensible snacks, preferably donated
Child-Friendly Tours	Up to $5	Potentially Free	• If your facility already offers guided tours, train your staff to take children on an exploratory tour wherein they get to ask the questions • Offer sensory objects throughout the tour that children can touch and feel, then relate those items to the museum's history and mission • Offer activities to be completed inside the facility, such as murals, crafts, or anything that incorporates technology

a beer fest or wine tasting; millennials are interested in creative, collaborative programming that offers unique experiences in an accessible and affordable environment. Refreshments might draw them in, but it is often the quality and originality of the programming itself that keeps them engaged. Affordable entry is just the starting point to crafting a real sense of community for millennials at your museum.

NOTES

1. Richard Fry, "5 facts about Millennial Households," Pew Research Center, Washington, D.C. (September 6, 2017), accessed December 8, 2017, http://www.pewre search.org/fact-tank/2017/09/06/5-facts-about-millennial-households/.

2. Elka Torpey and Andrew Hogan, "Working in a Gig Economy: Career Outlook: U.S. Bureau of Labor Statistics," May 2016, http://www.bls.gov/careeroutlook/2016/article/what-is-the-gig-economy.htm (accessed February 7, 2019).

3. Kristin Blagg, "The Rise of Master's Degrees: Master's Programs are Increasingly Diverse and Online," *Urban Institute*, December 2018, https://www.urban.org/sites/default/files/publication/99501/the_rise_of_masters_degrees_1.pdf (accessed March 7, 2019).

4. Larry Alton, "When the Gig Economy Is the Best and Worst Development for Workers Under 30," January 24, 2018, https://www.forbes.com/sites/larryalton/2018/01/24/why-the-gig-economy-is-the-best-and-worst-development-for-workers-under-30/ (accessed February 7, 2019).

5. Michael Hobbes, "FML: Why Millennials are Facing the Scariest Financial Future of Any Generation Since the Great Depression," *The Huffington Post*, https://highline.huffingtonpost.com/articles/en/poor-millennials-print/.

6. Geoffrey D. Paulin, "Fun Facts about Millennials: Comparing Expenditure Patterns from the Latest Through the Greatest Generation," Bureau of Labor Statistics, *Monthly Labor Review*, March 2018, https://www.bls.gov/opub/mlr/2018/article/fun-facts-about-millennials.htm (accessed March 7, 2019).

7. Geoffrey D. Paulin, "Fun Facts about Millennials: Comparing Expenditure Patterns from the Latest Through the Greatest Generation," Bureau of Labor Statistics, *Monthly Labor Review*, March 2018, https://www.bls.gov/opub/mlr/2018/article/fun-facts-about-millennials.htm (accessed March 7, 2019).

8. Geoffrey D. Paulin, "Fun Facts about Millennials: Comparing Expenditure Patterns from the Latest Through the Greatest Generation," Bureau of Labor Statistics, *Monthly Labor Review*, March 2018, https://www.bls.gov/opub/mlr/2018/article/fun-facts-about-millennials.htm (accessed March 7, 2019). This data reports the average

income to be $51,530.03 for members of the millennial generation versus $80,409.38 for members of generation X, the millennial predecessors.

9. Sarah O'Brien, CNBC, "Fed Survey Shows 40 Percent of Adults Still Can't Cover a $400 Emergency Expense," https://www.cnbc.com/2018/05/22/fed-survey-40 -percent-of-adults-cant-cover-400-emergency-expense.html.

10. Micah Solomon, *Forbes*, "For Small Business Week: All About Millennial Consumers and Millennial-Friendly Customer Experiences," https://www.forbes .com/sites/micahsolomon/2018/05/03/for-small-business-week-all-about-millennial -consumers-and-millennial-friendly-customer-experiences/#d1f0fcb2f91a.

11. Tina Wells, *Chasing Youth Culture and Getting it Right*, 45.

12. Tina Wells, *Chasing Youth Culture and Getting it Right*, 63.

13. Jeff Fromm and Marissa Vidler, *Millennials with Kids: Marketing to This Powerful and Surprisingly Different Generation of Parents* (New York: American Management Association, 2015), 48.

14. Colleen Dilenschneider, "Admission Discounts Negatively Impact Long Term Visitation (DATA)- Colleen Dilenschneider," *Know Your Own Bone* (blog), https:// www.colleendilen.com/2017/08/30/admission-discounts-negatively-impact-long -term-visitation-data/ (accessed June 1, 2018).

15. Colleen Dilenschneider, "Admission Discounts Negatively Impact Long Term Visitation (DATA)- Colleen Dilenschneider."

16. Colleen Dilenschneider, "Admission Discounts Negatively Impact Long Term Visitation (DATA)- Colleen Dilenschneider."

17. Raven Hudson (Millennial) in discussion with the author, May 2018.

18. Jennifer Lucy (Marketing Manager, Hermitage Museum and Gardens) in discussion with the author, May 2018. For more information on the Hermitage Museum and Gardens, visit their website at http://thehermitagemuseum.org/.

19. Jennifer Lucy, printed survey response given to author, May 18, 2018.

20. Jennifer Lucy (Marketing Manager, Hermitage Museum and Gardens) in discussion with the author, May 2018.

21. Andy Hahn (Executive Director, Campbell House Museum) in discussion with author, May 2018. For more information on the Campbell House Museum, visit their website at http://www.campbellhousemuseum.org/.

22. Andy Hahn (Executive Director, Campbell House Museum) in discussion with author, May 2018.

23. Jeff Fromm and Marissa Vidler, *Millennials with Kids*, 56.

3

U: "Uniqueness of Programming"

THIS chapter seeks to help museum professionals understand the types of museum programming millennials are likely to attend. Through an examination of available data sets and feedback from museum professionals, the chapter will outline what is considered "unique," why millennials value innovative programs, and examples of inventive programs museum professionals report as successful. This chapter will conclude with a discussion of millennial subsets and how the idea of uniqueness in programming applies to them.

WHAT MAKES PROGRAMMING UNIQUE?

Because I work for a small historic house museum, I am constantly trying to create or find the next captivating piece of programming. I try to find ways to take the narrative of my facility and highlight areas within it that are not usually our primary focus as an institution. These types of programs are then classified as unique for us simply because they are out of the norm.

In researching for this book, I expected to find that most historic house museums, which are unique by their very nature as time capsules of narrow and specific narratives, would already have fairly distinctive examples of programming already in place. Is it surprising that I found this was not the case? I spent hours, and sometimes days, perusing the annual event calendars of small historic house museums, only to discover to my dismay that we all seem to be following the same formula. To my disappointment, my museum also fits this description. We focus on the expected, not the unexpected. We offer themed tours, annual open houses, and holiday candlelight programs. We serve coffee in the morning, tea in the afternoon, and wine in the evening to make the experience feel more exclusive and special. Why are we cheapening the splendor of our sites by refusing to capitalize on the narratives that make each small museum different? We should be designing programs around those differences. I think this is the primary reason why millennials, despite their documented interest in local history and immersive experiences, are so often felt by museum professionals to be turning away from historic house museums. It is very possible we aren't taking enough risks in the content of our programming for them. We aren't being innovative enough. We are offering the same types of programs and expecting different results. The old adage that "if you build it, they will come" does not apply to this generation. They want different, they want valuable, they want unique. They want once-in-a-lifetime.

I am not suggesting that the formula that currently works for your institution needs to be thrown out; rather, I am advocating that museum professionals should consider modifying elements of existing programming and explore gaps in types of programming offered by the institution. Clearly, the admission data collected for attendance at your facility will offer an obvious indicator as to what works for you. If you are currently serving an older demographic, such as baby boomers, then please continue those programs. The issue museum professionals are facing now, though, is the idea that the millennial generation is underserved. This means that the types of programs millennials want or seek out are not being offered at a level comparable to their interest; and yes, the interest is there. Museum programming for this demographic is clearly lacking across the board, and with so many millennials interested in exploring our facilities, we would be remiss not to capitalize on this lack of options and fill the void with the immersive, innovative programs millennials crave.

Industry leader Colleen Dilenschneider also found evidence that diversifying the visitor experience through programming is a positive way to draw in a new, expanded audience. She explains, though, that museum professionals should not have the expectation that simply adding a new program, or creating a "one-off" as she terms it, will lead to success.[1] Instead, she ad-

FIGURE 3.1
Millennial at a Millennial Event
Created for Publication by Morven Moeller, 2018

vocates for crafting thoughtful and deliberate programs that align with your
museum's mission.[2] She states her article discussing this idea of diversifica-
tion is "about making your audiences' interests paramount, and connecting
them meaningfully to the values and mission of your organization."[3] Like
Colleen, I believe the key here is to begin with your mission as a museum
and find avenues to using that mission statement in creative and innovative
ways to implement programs that will prove authentic to your institution's
narrative. Beer and wine festivals have their places if they are relevant to
the museum's mission and what makes that facility original. Do you work
for a museum that was once home to a speakeasy? Then programming

focused on alcohol makes complete sense. Do you work for an institution that once served as a homestead and seeks to educate the public about farming practices? Then maybe you should find a more relevant way to reach out to a millennial audience than providing a wine tasting that is not necessarily authentic to your facility or its mission. You do not need to throw your mission statement out to engage millennials. Finding this balance is the key to determining how to use what makes your facility unique as a catalyst for bringing in a new or expanded audience.

WHY MILLENNIALS VALUE INNOVATION

Millennials identify with two phrases that emerged from pop culture in the 2010s, both which might seem ridiculous on paper but are extremely relevant to the millennial mindset. First, there is Y.O.L.O., which is an acronym for the phrase "you only live once." This acronym has its roots in a song by the popular music artist Drake and became an anthem for this generation to live their lives fully and without regrets.[4] The second is F.O.M.O., which is an acronym for the phrase "fear of missing out."[5] This phrase appeared in popular culture and piggybacked off of the popularity of Drake's call to action to lead a fulfilling life. These two acronyms genuinely reflect the deepest desires of the millennial generation. Studies show the most diagnosed mental illness of the past decade among young people is anxiety; they possess a literal fear of missing out on life.[6] This is reflected every single day in the choices they make regarding their time and money. Millennials will not waste either commodity on programs that are basic, that miss the mark, or are just plain average. They want, expect, and demand to fill their lives with experiences worthy of their time and money. If we want to attract them and keep their attention, we need to consistently evaluate the innovativeness of the programs we offer. We cannot settle for good enough. We must push the boundaries of our collective imaginations if we intend to engage this audience.

In order to gain further insight into the millennial mindset, I interviewed local historian and fellow millennial Joshua Weinstein. Joshua is plugged into the world around him, having worked with the Chrysler Museum of Art and as a board member for a local cemetery group. He has an educational background in the history field and is very involved in the development of the local arts scene in Norfolk, Virginia. His answers to my interview questions are pertinent to this discussion of why it is necessary to develop unique programs and whether or not millennials will come if they are created for them. I asked him how often he visits museums and his answer was almost immediate. "Whenever I am in a city that has one."[7] For Joshua, he can best experience the place he is in through the museums around him. He noted this is true for him in both his hometown and when he travels. I questioned him further as to what makes him decide to visit a specific facility. His answer was spot-on with what the research is telling museums and cultural institutions about the millennial obsession with time sensitivity and the fear of missing out. In fact, he actually used the phrase time sensitive in his answer. Joshua stated he usually asks himself the questions: "What will I not be able to see again? What is time-sensitive?"[8] He went on to explain "the special exhibit is usually the first thing I think of . . . tours are usually given every day, so they are not as valuable to me."[9] In fact, he stated tours are usually on the bottom of the list for him, unless they are given by an expert like a curator, a director, or an artist.[10] He desires the exclusive experience of being let in behind the curtain of the usual tours given by volunteers and docents.

Furthermore, Joshua discussed a facet of crafting programming that a few of my later interviews also revealed was important: access. When he discussed access, he suggested what felt the most special about museum programs he has attended was the feeling of being given special access. For Joshua, this was highlighted when he was at a conference and a reception held at a well-known large museum in Washington, D.C., and the attendees were given access to the facility after hours. They were allowed in locations usually either off-limits to the public or so crowded during business hours that it is impossible to enjoy the experience. This really stuck out for him as one of the best museum experiences of his lifetime. He noted the experience was tailored to the interests of his group, provided behind-the-scenes access, and allowed them in at nighttime.[11] All of these factors contributed to a feeling of exclusivity, which permeated the conversations I had with millennials throughout this research process and was frequently cited as one of the most vital factors they look for when choosing to visit a facility.

Textbox 3.1

"Museums need to create the illusion of exclusivity to draw in their audience." —Dustin Growick, Senior Creative Consultant, Museum Hack

For millennials, uniqueness is often synonymous with exclusivity. In chatting with Dustin Growick from Museum Hack, an industry leader in helping museums reset and rethink how they engage their audiences, it became evident that millennials want and expect the unusual in their programming. He said he likes to borrow a phrase from a colleague at Museum Hack that museums need to give the "illusion of exclusivity" to draw in a new audience.[12] He cited examples of facilities he has worked with, specifically in regard to how they were able to create this illusion. The key was to provide experiences that could be done in a small group, such as an escape room scenario.[13] By limiting the number of participants, it heightened the thrill of the experience. Additionally, being allowed to see behind the curtain or visit areas usually roped off to visitors are equally exciting options.[14] As long as the programming makes the participant feel like a member of an elite, small group, it is likely to have a positive impact on the millennial visitor.

The same is true with how millennials choose to engage as consumers. Studies of this generation of consumers have demonstrated that millennials are selective in the companies and institutions they choose to support. Aside from choosing to support those institutions which appear philanthropic or send messages of social importance, millennials often choose to patronize businesses with products that directly meet their needs and, more importantly, do so in innovative ways. For example, one particular group found that millennials are staunch advocates of rewards programs and are more likely to support businesses that have them in place.[15] This supports the idea that millennials value a feeling of exclusivity. Millennial shoppers are keen on rewards and loyalty programs because it puts them within an elite-like group of shoppers for a particular brand, which in turn also gives them access to greater discounts and a better shopping experience. This mindset can be applied to museums and cultural institutions as well.

Industry leaders are in an intense debate over whether or not millennials are interested in membership programs. I would argue millennials want to be part of membership programs, but only those that maintain active communication with them and meet their personal and financial needs. Additionally, when unique programming and once-in-a-lifetime experiences are offered through membership programs, millennials are more likely to join those programs.

A current trend among some art museums and larger cultural facilities is the addition of some sort of advisory board, which is generally comprised of members of the millennial generation and generation X. This trend seems to be fairly recent, with other nonprofit member-based organizations jumping on the bandwagon. This is an ideal avenue for engaging a millennial audience. By creating an advisory role for millennials interested in your facility, you are effectively inviting them to take an active and vested interest in the well-being of the museum. Additionally, it sends the very important message that your institution values being in relationship with millennials, which is a key component to maintaining their loyalty and interest. These groups can serve a variety of purposes, but should your team choose to implement one, giving voice to millennial ideas and concerns should be the cornerstone of its foundation. By allowing them a voice in the programming offered for them, they will likely do most of the difficult work of creating these unique experiences for you.

Maymont in Richmond, Virginia, engages millennials in this concept by allowing them a voice within the ranks of membership. They have created a level of their membership program known as the Dooley Noted Society, which consists of only young professionals. This group exists to "support Maymont through volunteer, social and fundraising activities."[16] They organize special programs on and off the property that are essentially designed by millennials and generation Xers for a young audience. They organize an annual Beer and Wine Classic and host socials at restaurants throughout the year to recruit others to help them support Maymont.[17] Their website noted a very creative event for 2018 meant to aid Maymont's Adopt-an-Animal program called Maymont's Turtle Races at Hardywood.[18] The event featured a local beer release and races between turtles that live at Maymont.[19] This was a great way to engage a millennial audience by offering facility-specific programming focused on a charitable cause. Maymont, and other institutions like it with membership levels and advisory boards made up of millennials, will continue to thrive with this younger demographic because of the relationships the organization has cultivated with them.

The Mystic Seaport Museum in Mystic, Connecticut, also incorporates the millennial voice in their programming through an informal millennial advisory board. Arlene Marcionette, the facility's Public Programs Project Manager, discussed what this board looks like and how it operates at length with me. She stated the group's objective is to help museum leadership brainstorm about events and activities that correlate with ongoing and forthcoming exhibits, determine logistics like pricing and times for events, and give perspective about what events might be well-received by a millennial audience.[20] These millennials, who number about thirty, meet almost quarterly as programs and seasons change and exhibits are changed out alongside them. For museum professionals interested in duplicating such a group, Arlene says she likes to keep the gatherings casual and brimming with pizza, snacks, and an open environment for discussion. In order to make the most of these planning sessions, the professionals overseeing the group need to ensure they provide the most detailed and up-to-date information possible for the group to work with; this means serious preparation.[21] This also sets the tone for the group to be able to manage expectations about what is realistic in planning programming around the exhibits.

Textbox 3.2

IN HER OWN WORDS: MILLENNIAL ADVISORY GROUPS

"We decided to start the group in the summer of 2017, as we embarked on planning a new event series aimed at young adults. This new event series would address several of our strategic plan goals: to establish Mystic Seaport Museum's identity as a cultural center that is contemporary, relevant, and essential to the community; to advance MSM's intellectual and experiential capacity; and to demonstrate the commitment of MSM to be a vibrant and inclusive community. We wanted to broaden our brand identity, increase visitation, and create experiences designed to have a lasting impact on the MSM community.

"One of our influences was an article in the March/April 2016 issue of *Museum* magazine titled, 'More than Just a Party: How the Isabella Stewart Gardner Museum Boosted Participation by Young Adults.' The article states that 'the museum's curator of education and public programs felt success hinged on allowing a group of people the same age as the target demographic to be in charge. They would have a natural understanding of how to reach the desired market.' We agreed that the best way to plan events that would appeal to young adults would be to engage that group directly, and have them tell us exactly what they want.

"The inaugural meeting took place on June 12, 2017, and we have held 5 additional meetings since that one. We do not meet on a regular schedule, but rather we get the group together about 2–3 months prior to an event we are planning (for this group, it's usually a Seaport After Seven event we are brainstorming, although sometimes the exercise triggers great ideas for other programs or activities at the museum). We meet after work (5:30–7pm) and have had an average of 8 attendees per meeting, mainly between the ages of 25–40. The members ebb and flow from meeting to meeting, but there are about 4–5 core members who attend almost all the meetings. In addition (although not counted in my numbers) are 2–3 non-millennial museum supervisors, and our Director of Exhibits.

"It began as 100% internal, and we've been able to pull in a few external members for the past 4 meetings. It was always the goal to have a mix of internal and external, but it's been a slowly building process since we've relied solely on word of mouth to draft outside members. The meetings are fairly structured; however the structure varies from meeting to meeting to keep things fresh. In a way, the meetings are events in and of themselves! We begin with introductions and an icebreaker game or activity. Thus far, all meetings have focused on one or more of our rotating exhibits, so we either give an overview of the exhibit or visit the exhibit if it's already open. Then we do a brainstorming activity and share ideas, which is always a fun and conversational part of the meeting. We might also run ideas by the group for music, food, price points, preferred days of the week, expectations around drinks, etc., and sometimes we hand out a survey. We provide snacks, and we offer everyone who attends the meeting a free ticket to the event.

"Each meeting has its own vibe depending on group dynamics and number of people. Light snacks seem to be more well-received than heavier food. I once brought a giant pizza that was hardly touched! In terms of "energy," we had a very successful meeting just last week. We moved around to a few different locations throughout the meeting (exhibit, summer camp room) and had snacks at the end while we shared out ideas. It felt very relaxed and convivial, which is definitely the atmosphere we are trying to promote.

"One thing I try to do either via email or in a subsequent meeting is to talk about the last event: how many of their ideas we were able to incorporate, how many people came to the event, etc. We want the group members to celebrate success with us, and feel joint ownership over the project. Occasionally one of the members will work the event, depending on their home department, but mainly we rely on the members for idea generation, and hopefully spreading the word among their circle of friends!"

—Arlene Marcionnette, Public Programs Project Manager, Mystic Seaport Museum (from email dated March 11, 2019)

You might wonder where Arlene and her staff found these millennials willing to participate in such an endeavor. She admits it began internally with the help of human resources. She had emails sent to those already involved in the museum who were within the desired demographic. Then, those who were interested gathered for the meetings. She is eager to expand outside the walls of the museum, and has been successful in recruiting other millennials through recommendations from colleagues or word of mouth. Some of these new recruits include millennials in their membership program, friends, and those involved in the local community.[22] Arlene and her colleagues are making great strides in incorporating the millennial voice.

I cannot advocate enough for having young people on your board in some capacity, especially if you feel lost as to where to start in adapting to marketing to this generation. Having a friend on the inside allows for your institution to

Textbox 3.3

"Our Millennial Advisory Board has proven to be a very useful tool . . . it allows us to work directly with millennials and respond to their needs and requests." —Arlene Marcionette, Public Programs Project Manager, Mystic Seaport Museum (in discussion with the author, August 2018)

be more effective in what it offers by limiting the constant guesswork of trying out different programs and hoping they succeed. You can set your facility up for success just by adding a few millennial voices to your ranks.

REAL-LIFE INVENTIVE MUSEUM PROGRAMS

Jeff Fromm and Marissa Vidler said it best:

"Millennials are enthusiastic seekers of the meaningfully unique, desiring something that connects them to your brand. In order to engage young adults, the conversation must be authentic and have a genuine connection to the everyday lifestyle of a young adult."[23]

The challenge is to create those unique experiences millennials crave, and to do so in a manner that is authentic to both the museum's mission and to the millennial experience. Unique programming will look different for each institution by its very definition. What works for one institution may not work for another, and the strengths of one institution will not always be present in another. To begin, museum professionals need to take a step back from their roles as insiders and view their sites as a first-time visitor. Then, ask yourself these questions:

- Look at the narrative your facility puts out to potential visitors. What are you promoting?
- Can you clearly identify your museum's mission from the advertising?
- Is there something in the mission, or in the collection itself, that is unique to the museum?
- How can the museum improve in promoting what makes it unique?

These might be tough questions to answer, and it is likely one of the reasons many facilities change their mission statement over time. They have to make a conscious effort to try to zero in on what makes the facility unique, necessary, and relevant. Some factors to consider when deciphering the aspects that make your museum unique could be:

- History of the facility
- Contents of the collection
- Location of the museum

In my position at the Hunter House Victorian Museum, we actively promote ourselves as the only Victorian house museum in Norfolk, Virginia. While our facility has many other interesting aspects to it, this is the primary face we show to our potential patrons. Why? We do this because it immediately sets us apart from our competition. If you are visiting Norfolk and want to tour a Victorian house, we are the only stop on the trail. This is a valuable position from which to market the facility and has helped us tremendously in our efforts since instituted in 2015. Prior to this point we were just another house museum; now we are the ONLY Victorian house visitors can tour.

In regard to programming, though, it is helpful to reach further into the concept of what is unique about your facility. I usually hone in on the concept that we are Victorian, and the only facility offering entirely Victorian programming in my immediate area. This means I can create programming around fundamentally Victorian concepts like Spiritualism and the ritual of afternoon tea. Additionally, the museum was the home of only one family and none of the children ever married or had children of their own, so visitors often find this to be a point of originality. Although, this is actually a prevalent narrative among historic house museums, the average tourist is not usually privy to this fact and is fascinated that the children never married and the family name died with them. We also celebrate the family with teas and programs specific to the parent's anniversary and children's birthdays. This is, after all, relevant only to us as a museum. Additionally, the Hunter family members were interested in genealogy and local history, so we use that fact to partner with neighboring facilities concerned with those subjects, such as the local archives and heritage organizations. This partnership led us to one of our most successful events of 2017.

Our most successful event of 2017, in terms of attracting a large number of people and cultivating a new audience, most of whom were millennials, was our inaugural 19th Century Scavenger Hunt. This program was a passion project of mine that developed after I attended the Southeastern Museum Conference in 2016 and heard from a panelist discussing the use of Instagram to engage audiences. (Conferences really are worth the registration fee!) The panelist discussed a virtual scavenger hunt that was being done in Atlanta. The program creatively used Instagram to encourage participants to take pictures of the places as they discovered them and then use a museum-specific hashtag to promote the event. It sounded like a genius idea to me, and I knew I needed to try to implement one in Norfolk.

Fortunately in 2017 I had two skilled interns for the job. We partnered with the Slover Library's Sargent Memorial Collection, which is Norfolk's local archive, to complete the project. The concept was simple: create a scavenger hunt that began at the library and ended at the museum and included stops at relevant historic buildings along the way. Participants used a printed booklet with a map and information on all of the stops along the walk to find the buildings, some of which were no longer standing and had been replaced with modern architecture. They were then instructed to find the corresponding picture from the sleeve of printed images they were given, hold it up to the spot where the building either was or would have been standing, and take a picture. Once completed, these were uploaded by the participants to Instagram and Facebook with a hunt-specific hashtag. In a brilliant effort by all parties involved, we created one hundred scavenger hunt packets including the booklets and printed pictures for social media use. The event was open to participants from 9 a.m. to 5 p.m. on a Saturday in October. We required preregistration to ensure we had enough packets as well as gift bags and refreshments for those who completed the hunt. To our surprise, the event attracted nearly four hundred participants, most of whom had never visited our facility before. To date, this has been the most well attended event hosted by the museum. For the event at-a-glance, see textbox 3.4.

Textbox 3.4

Event Highlight: 19th Century Scavenger Hunt

Facility: Hunter House Victorian Museum

Location: Norfolk, Virginia

Budget: <$200,000

Staff Size: 3 paid, plus volunteers

Event Description: "Presented by the Hunter House Victorian Museum and the Sargeant Memorial Collection at the Slover Library, the Historic Norfolk Scavenger Hunt allows participants to explore the city of Norfolk through the eyes of the Hunter family as you experience the world they knew at the turn of the twentieth century! Begin your journey at the Slover Library, where instructions can be picked up, and end your quest at the Hunter House Victorian Museum with a first-floor open house, light refreshments and a finishers' bag! Participants will receive a guidebook of information, designed by Hunter House interns, detailing the history of each building with corresponding photographs and illustrations provided by the Sargeant Memorial Collection at the Slover Library. To complete the scavenger hunt, teams will walk the path of the Hunter family, identifying designated historical buildings along the way using the guidebook. Teams will then take a photograph of each building overlapping the historic photograph over the existing structure. Along the way, be sure to use social media and the tag #HistoricNorfolk to track your progress as you locate each building and document your findings." (Taken directly from the Facebook event page at https://www .facebook.com/events/166754340561273/.)

Average Attendance: 400

Ways Marketed: Social media platforms, Eventbrite ticketing website, Slover Library

Director's Take: "This event allowed my facility to capitalize on what makes us unique and collaborate with local businesses to draw in new audiences from the community." —Jaclyn Spainhour (author), Director

Why It Works: This event offers a free, unique experience for locals in the community to explore a new facet of their surroundings. It seamlessly combined the missions of both the museum and the archives while incorporating an interactive, educational experience for participants. This event was most successful with young families who homeschooled their children and small groups of millennials who enjoyed the thrill of the hunt together. The event materials were mostly funded by the library and the museum provided the refreshments. Finishers' bags were filled with items donated by local businesses. The added hashtag offered a technological component millennials expect and allowed for free, consumer-endorsed advertising for the facility.

What made the scavenger hunt successful was the amount of participation, specifically from a brand-new audience. We did not charge for this event, although we are considering charging a nominal $5 fee per group for upcoming hunts to cover the cost of materials. If you were to decide to implement something similar, you could always ask a board member to sponsor the event or apply for a grant to cover the costs. The biggest measure of success from our perspective was the sheer number of first-time visitors we received at the finish line. The museum was the last stop on the hunt and participants were welcomed into our garden to have a refreshment and receive their prizes for completing, which consisted of promotional goods and coupons donated by local businesses. We opened our doors for free that day to anyone who completed the hunt, but they were not given a guided tour (we all should know after the last chapter that this cheapens the experience). The return rate in 2018 for participants from the hunt has been a measurable success. We included $1 off admission coupons in their prize bags and have seen many make their way back to the museum. Best of all, people are still talking about it and asking for us to do another. This has become something we can do annually and provides a valuable internship experience each summer for two of the museum's interns, who are usually millennials. In 2018, our interns are working on the theme of exploring nineteenth-century Norfolk through a child's eyes, an idea we chose because many millennials and their children attended the hunt in 2017. Most parents commented on the educational value of the experience and that they would come annually if it was offered. Based on our records, a large number of these participants have returned for regular paid tours and special programming. Opening your museum up to engage in a community-based event like this scavenger hunt may be a great way for your museum to diversify its audience. For us, it was a remarkable success.

For your facility, the narrative may be completely different. You may work for an art museum, or a museum of toy cars, or a town's history museum. Whatever the narrative of your museum, you can use these questions to help you think about the purpose of your facility and what makes it original. The answers should help the museum professionals on your team craft programming that is specific to the facility and unique enough to attract a millennial audience.

There are also programs that your staff may have designed for another audience that would work well for a millennial audience if tweaked to meet their needs. One example comes from Jill Hartz, the Executive Director of the Jordan Schnitzer Museum of Art in Eugene, Oregon. Her museum's mission is to assist students at the University of Oregon and to use its collection to round out their learning experience. Jill knew there were new ways to make art relevant to her student audience, who are currently part of the generation after the millennial generation, which is sometimes referred to as generation Z. She decided to use her facility to take on an innovative approach to incorporating the common reading of the university with museum's art museum by designing exhibits around the central themes of the year's chosen work. It is also important to note here that a student advisory board was used to select the work for each year, which allowed them to actively participate and have a vested interest in the project.[24] The topics and featured art change each year as the common reading changes, but each year the topics highlighted speak to the student audience. Thus far, exhibits have showcased art on the themes of identity, immigration, sexual boundaries, and more. These topics are relevant to this audience, who are coming into adulthood and faced with these ideas in their daily lives.

Textbox 3.5

Event Highlight: Common Reading—Common Seeing

Facility: Jordan Schnitzer Museum of Art, University of Oregon

Location: Eugene, Oregon

Staff Size: 32 paid employees

Budget: $4 million (Large Museum)

Event Description: "This academic year, all UO first-year students received Louise Erdrich's novel *The Round House*; faculty are using the book in courses across campus for undergraduate and graduate students. Last year, more than sixty classes used the museum's first exhibition organized specifically to support the 'Common Reading.' Based on the success of Between the World and Me: African American Artists Respond to Ta-Nehisi Coates, the JSMA plans to present a 'Common Seeing' exhibition each year—where students can expand their dialogues and investigations in front of works of art. This year's

---

companion exhibition, Conversations in the Round House: Roots, Roads and Remembrances, features twenty-four contemporary works by twelve artists who affirm their ties to Native culture: Rick Bartow, Ka'ila Farrell-Smith, Joe Feddersen, James Lavadour, Tanis Matthews, P. Y. Minthorn, Lillian Pitt, Jaune Quick-to-See Smith, Wendy Red Star, Gail Tremblay, Marie Watt, and Elizabeth Woody. The majority of the objects come from the JSMA's collection, and some works, like James Lavadour's painting *Torch*, are recent acquisitions on exhibition for the first time here. We are also grateful to the artists and private collectors who lent their important works. The exhibition addresses central concerns in Erdrich's novel—community and identity, landscape and a sense of place, and history, memory and storytelling, as well as violence to women, sovereignty, justice, and racism. The novel begins with the rape of the narrator's mother, which starts the adolescent son on a journey that makes him question social mores, sacred rituals, and his place on the reservation and in the larger world. Likewise, the works in the exhibition explore the diverse ways artists approach cultural heritage, freedom and colonization, and the uneasy coexistence of natural, material and spiritual worlds. Conversations in the Round House: Roots, Roads and Ritual is co-curated by Danielle Knapp, McCosh Associate Curator, and Cheryl Hartup, Associate Curator of Academic Programs and Latin American Art with Beth Robinson-Hartpence (Lenni Lenape), JSMA art preparator-conservator, who advised on the project."
(Pulled directly from https://jsma.uoregon.edu/RoundHouse)

Average Attendance: 760 students from 30 classes

Ways Marketed: Social media platforms, website, member materials, around campus, some paid advertising on the radio, and in print

Director's Take: "It offers the primary audience—students—ways to visualize themes of identity, culture, history, and other topics specific to the book itself. Students are particularly interested in exploring their own identities and how they negotiate their being in the world, and the books are chosen to appeal to first-year students." —Jill Hartz, Executive Director

Why It Works: We know millennials want to find their place in the world, and while this event is not geared toward millennials, it could be tweaked to do so. This event worked well for its student audience because it allowed them to find themselves within the pages of the common reading assignments given by the university. It created a commonality among all students that promoted camaraderie as well as self-discovery. The ways it was marketed focused on the student population and made the impact it intended to make. With faculty support of the exhibit, the event became even more successful as they discovered art could be used to support the learning objectives of the classes using the common reading.

When asked, Jill described the project this way:

Because our Common Seeing supports and extends dialogue that's critical to the Common Reading, it offers the primary audience—students—ways to visualize themes of identity, culture, history, and other topics specific to the book itself. Students are particularly interested in exploring their own identities and how they negotiate their being in the world, and the books are chosen to appeal to first-year students.

The JSMA aims to be one of the finest teaching museums in our nation, and we work with most schools and colleges and more than 40 departments across campus to integrate art into their curricula. Last year, more than 9,000 university students and more than 5,000 K–12 students came to the museum for academic purposes. We also partner with student groups on our exhibition projects and special events and have a student membership organization that further integrates the museum into student life.

Three years ago, when we started the Common Seeing, responding to Coates's book *Between the World and Me*, we were taking a chance that faculty would bring their students to the gallery to see how works by Glenn Ligon, Kara Walker, Theaster Gates, Rashid Johnson, and others would make visible how the author negotiates being a Black man in the world, and especially in the U.S. We don't have a large African American student population in Oregon, so we were glad that the exhibition resonated with a number of African American students who began to hang out in the gallery and engage visitors with the works themselves. When asked, some said they felt seen and safe in the space and knowing that the artists we featured were among the most prominent and respected in the country, made them proud of their heritage.[25]

Her passion for this project is evident, and its success ultimately hinged, as she pointed out, on students being able to identify with the topics. By making students see themselves in the exhibits, the staff made the work and the highlighted pieces of art relevant to the viewers. This type of project could be easily adapted to a millennial audience, who also share this need to find their own identities and places in the world. Museum professionals could develop exhibits around new literary works which featured much of the same central themes that are important to millennials: identity, racism, sexuality, mental health, and more. These programs could also be adapted to serve many other audiences. Jill suggests senior citizen groups, book clubs, and community groups.[26] A project like this requires a willingness to research your audience and find out what is important to them. With the help of this book, you should feel comfortable identifying those topics and moving forward on a distinct version of this unique and innovative project.

WILL MILLENNIALS COME?

One of the interviews I conducted in gathering information on programming for this book really stopped me in my tracks. I was interviewing a historic house museum professional and had begun asking my series of questions regarding what the interviewee thinks about the millennial generation and how their facility serves this demographic. When I asked my usual question of what comes to mind when this person hears the term millennial, I was given a mostly negative answer. At this point, I had conducted over a dozen interviews and had yet to encounter someone with a negative characterization of the generation. I followed up with the question of whether the facility offered programs designed for millennials. The answer was a swift no, followed by a few words that really stuck with me: why have programs for them if they won't come?

Textbox 3.6

"I visit museums whenever I am in a city that has one." —Joshua Weinstein, 33

The person being interviewed was a baby boomer, and after speaking with this person for almost an hour, I came to realize the negativity actually came from a place of confusion; confusing notions of who millennials are, what they really want, and how to communicate with a generation almost always attached to technology. We had a very productive conversation and eventually discovered together that, although this person initially reported millennials hardly ever attended and were not interested in the facility, actually millennials made up quite a decent sector of visitors for specific programs. Millennials attended events hosted by this facility that offered opportunities to dress up, socialize, and immerse themselves in the atmosphere of the museum. I am including this anecdote for those that need to hear it again: millennials DO want to visit your facility. You likely already have some type of unique programming in place that is attractive to millennials. Improving upon your current programs can only help your organization move upward.

Another method of drawing in millennials to your facility that will provide them that feeling of exclusivity is allowing them to participate in the behind-the-scenes work of your museum. This could take a variety of forms. Some facilities choose to offer tours with someone of note, such as the Director or the Curator. This usually fares well for art museums offering time-sensitive exhibits, or museums with very generalized tours that become more in-depth

---

Textbox 3.7

QUICK TIP: GENERATE MORE INTEREST

Not seeing the interest level from millennials you want to in your programs? Consider your method of advertisement and the content of your descriptions. Use buzz words like unique, discover, immerse, celebrate, and others indicative of an interactive or otherwise worthwhile experience. Social media and online advertising are key to launching a successful campaign for marketing your event. Create a Facebook event, put links in your Instagram biography, and place online ads in places that matter. For print materials, send someone to post vibrant, catchy fliers in coffee shops, bookstores, popular brunch locations, and shops frequented by millennials. Whenever possible, find a millennial to do the placement; they know the popular spots in your town or city.

when led by a senior museum professional. Other museums offer literal tours of areas usually off limits to patrons, and often in small groups to make the experience feel even more special. One example of an institution which offers such programming is Maymont in Richmond, Virginia. Maymont Mansion is supported by the Maymont Foundation and the two entities work in tandem to provide educational and immersive experiences to the public. They offer behind-the-ropes tours of the facility to give visitors a more personal and detailed experience of the mansion.[27] These experiences are not unique, but the information provided on these tours allows visitors to feel like they have been given special access, which is important to a millennial audience.

One of my favorite trends surfacing among museums around the country are interactive experiences focused on team building and problem solving, both of which are characteristic of millennials.[28] This takes many innovative forms, two of the most popular being murder mysteries and escape rooms. No longer do people have to purchase murder mysteries in a box and host guests in their homes; they can come to the museum. Add in costumes, music, character interactions, and refreshments and millennials will be beating down the door to get in. Millennials respond well to these programs because they support teamwork and collaborative learning, which are hallmarks of the generation as a whole.[29] Escape rooms are just as popular, especially because museum professionals can theme them specifically for the mission and contents of their museum. Secret passages and puzzles can be added to just about any theme and feel authentic to the facility. These events also play into the concept described by Jeff Fromm and Marissa Vidler that millennials crave adventure, specifically safe forms of adventure.[30] Escape rooms and murder mysteries certainly provide that atmosphere. The bonus of this experience is it provides that feeling of exclusivity by admitting small groups, one at a time. The murder mystery experience can also feel exclusive by ensuring those running the event spread out the characters across the facility and limit the number of participants for each program. To make the most of the effort put into the event, museum professionals can create photo opportunities for participants that will aid in expanding the impact of the program. These photos can then be uploaded, hash tagged, and shared across social media. It is a great opportunity for free advertising and will help the museum reach more of the millennial demographic organically. Free, honest, patron-driven advertising should always be the aim of your marketing team. Millennials respond well to this type of advertising because it feels authentic. In this case, if you build it, and others in the generation positively promote it, they likely will come.

PRACTICAL APPLICATIONS

In summation, creating unique or exclusive programming is one the most effective ways to engage a millennial audience at your facility. Millennials value uniqueness because they are focused, as a generation, on the concept that time is limited and should be spent on experiences that simply cannot be missed. Effective advertising draws in the group by pointing to facts about the programs offered that make them appear as if they are limited in some way, whether that be in ticket availability, number of showings of a program, or time sensitivity.

When considering how to market to subgroups of millennials, it is important first to acknowledge generally what is unique about your facility and its contents. Once you have determined what the selling point is for your facility, then you can begin to use that concept as the foundation for your programming. The idea itself of what constitutes unique programming does not differ significantly between millennials in relationships and childless millennials. What will attract both groups is your ability as a team of museum professionals to illustrate to them why they should put your museum at the top of their to-do list. For both groups, time sensitivity will likely prove an attractive incentive to visit. If there is an exhibit featuring artwork from a contemporary artist that is only on display for three months, it is likely this exhibit will get more foot traffic than a year-long exhibit simply because there is that fear of missing it entirely because of the short window of opportunity presented by the facility. If the museum were to then have a one-night only meet and greet with the artist, that event could expect to fare even better because the event will only take place for a few hours and will likely not be repeated. This feeling of needing to have these time-sensitive experiences appeals to the millennial audience because it feeds off of their collective fear of missing out on life. The experiences provided by escape rooms, murder mysteries, and exclusive costumed events also reflect this same mindset. This feeling plays into the decision-making process for all subgroups of millennials, but is usually secondary for the millennials with children, who tend to place the wants and needs of their children over their own.

It is vital to continue to emphasize this fact: there is simply too much competition for the attention of children at museums. It is, of course, fundamental to almost everyone's mission that the museum provide education for children. Most accomplish this by offering tours and programs for school groups and the like, which is absolutely necessary and vital to your institution's sense of credibility in the community. However, outside of programs for the school system, the programs offered by museums are fairly standard. There are story times, crafts, and outdoor activities. The market for introducing children's programming is flooded and for it to be successful for your facility, you really have to offer something so unique that it cannot be found within a five-mile radius. I will not even attempt to touch summer camps at my facility, both because the market is flooded and because my staffing is limited and primarily volunteer. Instead, I have chosen to institute two avenues of programming for children that are considered to be unique to my area.

The first is a children's membership program designed for ages four to ten. The program is extremely affordable at $30 per child per year, with discounts for multiple children, and entitles them to attend the twelve events each year scheduled specifically for the children's membership program. They also get free tours for the calendar year, discounts in our shop, and a special birthday surprise mailed to them. This year the birthday surprise was a charm of the museum for the girls and coloring books for the boys. The types of programs vary in type, but all directly relate to my museum's mission to educate patrons on the subject of nineteenth-century culture. Space is limited, which also has helped increase participation since the millennial parents feel it is an exclusive experience for their child. In 2018 we offered programs like:

- Victorian parlor games
- Vintage valentines
- Peter Rabbit story time and egg hunt
- Victorian field day
- Blue Willow tea
- Teddy bear sleepover

Parents are given the full schedule when they sign up and are asked to register for each event, all of which occur on either a Saturday or Sunday to encourage attendance. This program has proven successful for us in a couple of ways. First, we now have a solid base of a few dozen children who engage with us regularly and will likely grow up with our facility. Secondly, the parents are now invested in the facility and many have become museum members themselves to continue to support our ability to provide these types of programs for their children. Lastly, the advertising for these programs has allowed our facility to be seen as welcoming to children, which is often a difficult task for historic houses due to the fragility of our collections and our typical "don't touch" policy. While this is not a financially lucrative program for my museum, the investment we make in the program is worth the cost because it is putting us on the map as a facility with unique children's programming in our area. For information on this children's membership program at-a-glance, see table 3.1.

Textbox 3.8

CRAFTING STORY TIME

Thinking of starting a story time at your museum? Take these steps to create a successful program. First, pick a day and time that does not compete with the facilities around you. Competition is not a good thing in this flooded market. Second, do not charge for the program. Save the fundraising for the adults. Lastly, get creative! Hand-pick books related to your museum's mission or find a character to do the readings. Make your facility stand out—and don't forget to advertise on social media!

The second type of programming that has worked well for my museum is our story time. Yes, the market is flooded with these kinds of events, but if your facility can take an interesting spin on the classic story time then it is worth doing. If you are considering starting a story time at your facility, the first step should be to check out your competition. First, be sure to note when other museums in your area are hosting their story times. If possible, work around those days and times. Millennial parents, especially those who are homeschooling their children, often plan their weekly calendars around these mostly free educational events. It is likely your facility will get more traffic if you are not competing with another museum offering a comparable program

Table 3.1. Children's Membership Program

Event Offered as Benefit of Membership (no cost to participant)	Description	Cost to Museum	Tips
Afternoon Teas	In a calendar year, two teas were offered. The first was a Blue Willow Tea which discussed English transferware and the second was a Paper Doll Tea which discussed crafts in the nineteenth century. Tea, sweets, and savories were provided for the children as well as a craft.	Under $40 per event (based on 12 children)	• Pick topics unique to your facility • Use inexpensive materials for the crafts (for the Blue Willow Tea, we used paper plates and construction paper cutouts to let children design their own transferware) • Ask for donations for refreshments
Fun and Games	In a calendar year, three events were offered that were based within this category. First were traditional parlor games inside the museum parlor. Second was a Victorian field day featuring nineteenth-century outdoor recreation. Third was a Fall Festival featuring pumpkin decorating, bobbing for apples, and other outdoor games.	Under $40 per event (based on 12 children)	• Try to use materials the museum already owns, or choose games that require few physical items like charades • Shop at the local dollar store when able, or ask your volunteers to loan items for outdoor play • Ask for donations for refreshments
Letters from Home	This event was offered once and done in conjunction with a local navy wife who was collecting items for Taste of Home care packages. The museum provided coloring book pages for the youngest children and letter writing materials for the older children to express their thanks.	Potentially Free	• Print pages offline of patriotic scenes for children to color—check for a copyright! • Have colorful pens and plenty of paper for the older children • Use promotional postcards when able • Ask for donations for refreshments
Story Time and Egg Hunt	This event was offered at Eastertime and featured a story time with Peter Rabbit readings, an Easter egg hunt, and light refreshments. Eggs and candy were provided by museum volunteers, as were the refreshments.	Potentially Free	• Ask volunteers to donate candy, eggs, and refreshments (check for allergies) • Be sure to separate the children into two groups—the older children typically get all the eggs before the young ones find one

(continued)

Table 3.1. Continued

Event Offered as Benefit of Membership (no cost to participant)	Description	Cost to Museum	Tips
Teddy Bear Sleepover	This event allowed children to drop off their favorite toy for a night of adventure at the museum. Staff photographed the toys having a blast overnight and the children returned in the morning to view the photos, have a snack, and read a story about an adventurous stuffed bear.	Potentially Free	• Arrange for drop-off on a Friday afternoon and include time for working parents to make the deadline—we picked 3–7 p.m. • Purchase photo paper and print off images for each child to take home as a memento—if you are in a pinch, create a slideshow of images and email them to all the parents • Ask for a volunteer to read the story, and ask for donations of cookies and lemonade for snack
Day in Fairyland	This event featured a volunteer Queen of the Fairies who read a story, facilitated games, and helped the children create fairy gardens. The gardens consisted of small clay pots filled with soil and decorated with dollar store finds like beads, stones, figurines, and ribbons. Each child was provided with fairy wings and refreshments as well.	Under $50 (based on 12 children)	• All items should be purchased at a discount store for the fairy gardens (we also purchased the wings at one as well) • Choose a volunteer with plenty of patience—the children have limited attention spans! (Ours chose to play tag most of the afternoon) • Ask for donations for refreshments
Victorian Valentines/ Stamping Thanks	This event was held for Valentine's Day and Thanksgiving, and allowed children to use lace doilies, paper, stamps, ink, and stickers to create vintage valentines and thank-you cards. Refreshments were also provided.	Under $20 per event (based on 12 children)	• Have volunteers donate craft supplies • Ask for donations for refreshments • Shop at the discount store as needed
Cocoa with Mrs. Claus	This event offered children a morning story time with a character and included refreshments of cookies and cocoa.	Potentially Free	• Find a volunteer, whether from your institution or from a local theater group, to play Mrs. Claus • Ask for donations for refreshments

on a similar day and time. Second, make the event free. With children, it is vital to note that their collective attention span is often limited and parents do not want to pay $10 to come to something Johnny will only sit through for five minutes. As is custom, feel free to suggest a donation price, but do not charge for these events. They should be considered essential to your mission and not part of your fundraising efforts. Lastly, think about what you have identified that makes your facility unique and use that to craft your story time. For my museum, this meant having one of my volunteers dress up as a governess to do story time in our garden once weekly. We have been running this program during the summertime and attendance fluctuates based on the weather, but interest is steady. Our governess acts as a fictitious member of the household and the volunteer actress who plays her has created a character, accent and all, for the children to engage. This program has proven quite successful because of the governess component. I am confident this would not be the case if there was not a character or some other type of "spin" that made this program feel fun and different. Each museum has something that makes it special; use that concept as the foundation for turning regular, expected programming into creative, enticing programming.

Take the time to really dissect what is original about your facility and use those aspects to diversify your audience through creative, immersive programming. Millennials celebrate diversity and will react well to your institution's willingness to take what makes it unique and translate that idea into tangible experiences. Take advantage of the millennial interest in community involvement and volunteerism and give their ideas a voice within the ranks of your facility. By doing so, you will have an engaged and satisfied millennial audience for years to come.

NOTES

1. Colleen Dilenschneider, "From Happy Hours to Fun Runs: How to Successfully Diversify the Visitor Experience (DATA)- Colleen Dilenschneider," *Know Your Own Bone* (blog), https://www.colleendilen.com/2017/12/06/leisure-affinity-potential-visitors-not-visit-data/ (accessed June 30, 2018).

2. Colleen Dilenschneider, "From Happy Hours to Fun Runs: How to Successfully Diversify the Visitor Experience (DATA)- Colleen Dilenschneider."

3. Colleen Dilenschneider, "From Happy Hours to Fun Runs: How to Successfully Diversify the Visitor Experience (DATA)- Colleen Dilenschneider."

4. Leor Galil, "Does Drake Own YOLO?", https://www.forbes.com/sites/leor
galil/2012/12/29/does-drake-own-yolo/#3ed6302f2556, Last modified December 29,
2012 (accessed November 12, 2017).

5. Ben Scheckinger, "The Home of FOMO," https://www.bostonmagazine.com/
news/2014/07/29/fomo-history/, last modified July 29, 2014 (accessed November 11,
2017).

6. Jia Tolentino, "Where Millennials Come From: And Why We Insist on Blaming
Them for It," https://www.newyorker.com/magazine/2017/12/04/where-millennials
-come-from, last modified December 4, 2017 (accessed June 20, 2018).

7. Joshua Weinstein (Millennial) in discussion with the author, June 2018.

8. Joshua Weinstein (Millennial) in discussion with the author, June 2018.

9. Joshua Weinstein (Millennial) in discussion with the author, June 2018.

10. Joshua Weinstein (Millennial) in discussion with the author, June 2018.

11. Joshua Weinstein (Millennial) in discussion with the author, June 2018.

12. Dustin Growick (Senior Creative Consultant, Museum Hack) in discussion
with the author, June 2018. For more information on Museum Hack, visit https://
museumhack.com/.

13. Dustin Growick (Senior Creative Consultant, Museum Hack) in discussion
with the author, June 2018.

14. Dustin Growick (Senior Creative Consultant, Museum Hack) in discussion
with the author, June 2018.

15. Christopher Donnelly and Renato Scaff, "Who are the Millennial Shoppers?
What Do They Really Want?" *Outlook* 2 (2013), https://www.accenture.com/us-en/
insight-outlook-who-are-millennial-shoppers-what-do-they-really-want-retail (accessed June 20, 2018).

16. "Dooley Noted Society-Maymont," https://maymont.org/support/membership/
dooley-noted-society/, last modified 2018 (accessed June 30, 2018).

17. "Dooley Noted Society-Maymont," https://maymont.org/support/membership/
dooley-noted-society/, last modified 2018 (accessed June 30, 2018).

18. "Dooley Noted Society-Maymont," https://maymont.org/support/membership/
dooley-noted-society/, last modified 2018 (accessed June 30, 2018).

19. "Dooley Noted Society-Maymont," https://maymont.org/support/membership/
dooley-noted-society/, last modified 2018 (accessed June 30, 2018).

20. Arlene Marcionette (Public Programs Project Manager, Mystic Seaport Museum) in discussion with the author, August 2018. For more information on the Mystic Seaport Museum, visit https://www.mysticseaport.org/.

21. Arlene Marcionette (Public Programs Project Manager, Mystic Seaport Museum) in discussion with the author, August 2018.

22. Arlene Marcionette (Public Programs Project Manager, Mystic Seaport Museum) in discussion with the author, August 2018.

23. Fromm and Vidler, *Millennials with Kids*, 89.

24. Jill Hartz, email message to author, March 30, 2019.

25. Jill Hartz, email message to author, March 30, 2019.

26. Jill Hartz, email message to author, March 30, 2019.

27. Kathy Alcaine (Senior Manager of Programs and Interpretation, Maymont) in discussion with the author, June 2013. For more information on Maymont, visit http:// maymont.org.

28. Howe and Strauss, *Millennials Rising*, 44.

29. Howe and Strauss, *Millennials Rising*, 155.

30. Fromm and Vidler, *Millennials with Kids*, 3.

R: "Relevance"

THIS chapter seeks to discuss how museum professionals can ensure the programming offered at their respective institutions is relevant to both the museum's mission statement and the interests of a millennial audience. First, this chapter will define what relevance means to millennials and how to identify areas of relevancy for this audience. Next, this chapter will discuss why remaining relevant to the museum's mission is a vital element in the creation of programming. This chapter will also examine how the idea of relevance differs between millennial subgroups. By the end of this chapter, museum professionals should be able to understand the idea of relevance, why it is an important factor in developing museum programming, and how the concept of relevance is tied to a millennial audience.

DEFINING RELEVANCE FOR A MILLENNIAL AUDIENCE

The word "relevant" is a loaded term, and generalizing it for an entire generation is a difficult task. Relevance often seems like personalization, but that is not always the case. Being relevant can mean everything from being current to adhering to specific ideals and beliefs. It really is an ambiguous term, and not just for museums and cultural organizations. Colleen Dilenschneider explains the importance of this idea when discussing millennials and visitation to museums, stating "relevance may be prerequisite for engagement of any kind."[1]

She is completely correct; without relevant programming, museum professionals cannot expect initial or continuing millennial engagement.

For the purposes of this discussion, relevance will be defined by being broken into two categories: highlighting modern social issues and creating a feeling of nostalgia. While these two categories appear paradoxical, they adequately characterize the concerns and needs of the millennial generation. From previous chapters and discussions, we already know that millennials place importance on social advocacy and make great strides to support institutions with similar values. This can mean supporting local businesses, helping eradicate global issues, or rallying for equal rights across the boundaries of gender and sexuality. In a museum setting, it is important to recognize that millennials are viewing the world both from the perspective of their life thus far as well as through the lens of "now." Their museum experiences are a result of their collective memories, likes, and dislikes meeting their current concerns and sense of advocacy. Museum professionals around the country are implementing exhibits highlighting many of those current issues that are relevant to today's millennials. In my own hometown, an area art museum recently exhibited works by a contemporary artist meant to spark discussion about mental illness and beauty. Studies show millennials are currently the most anxious generation, and I can personally attest that in my circle of millennial professionals and friends at least two-thirds are either medicated or seeking therapy for anxiety, depression, and related mental illnesses, including me. As a result, the subject of mental illness acceptance and awareness is a hot topic for my generation. Museums like my local art museum are smart to capitalize on this topic by creating an exhibit around it. This is what it looks like for a museum to be relevant to the millennial generation.

The other side of advocacy is focused on current hot-button issues that affect millennials, such as

- Equal pay for women in the workplace
- Paid maternity and paternity leave
- LGBTQ rights
- Immigration
- Societal inclusion across races and ethnicities
- Mental health

Museum professionals are, generally speaking, making great strides in modeling what it means to be inclusive, pro-parent, and pro self-identity. Many institutions are making changes at a human resources level, but the real question is: does your institution lead by example, both internally and externally? What face does your institution put out to the world? If your promotional materials are filled with middle-aged, white, childless individuals, you likely know your museum is missing the mark. Millennials, like most people, want to see themselves reflected in the programs geared toward them. If they are able to identify themselves in your promotional campaigns, they are likely to find your institution relevant. This relevance can be accomplished on a base level by ensuring your team is made up of an eclectic group of people from various backgrounds. A thirty-year-old African American man considering visiting a museum whose staff is comprised of middle-aged white women and whose promotional materials only highlight women with children may not see himself reflected in the offerings of that museum, and therefore not find the institution relevant. It is vital for museum professionals to diversify their portfolios, front-of-the-house staff, and social media presences to reflect the demographic they want to attract. As a generation who demonstrably values diversity and inclusion, millennials will appreciate museums that give the appearance of eclecticism in their marketing and follow through with that appearance and make it a reality when they visit.

Not all museum professionals are able to take advocacy on as a theme for programming. This is often the case with museums and cultural institutions affiliated with larger political or government entities, colleges and universities,

---

Textbox 4.1

DIVERSITY MATTERS TO MILLENNIALS

Diversify your audience by diversifying your marketing; make your museum relevant by helping millennials see themselves reflected in your marketing efforts. Millennials value diversity and inclusion and will respect your institution more when those concepts are valued by your museum.

and other governing bodies. Often, these institutions are directly prohibited from advocating due to these affiliations. But just because you and your colleagues may not be able to rally at a minority rights convention wearing your museum name badges and polo shirts does not mean that you cannot make a difference and remain relevant to a millennial audience in other ways that promote inclusion and education. For example, Matt Davis, the Director of Historic Museums for Georgia College, described themed tours his staff gives on the subjects of slavery and women's roles at one of the institution's properties called the Governor's Mansion.[2] These tours are given separately from the normal tours at the facility and are specialized by subject. Each tour offers more in-depth information regarding race relations and the roles of women, both white women and women of color, during the nineteenth century.[3] Such tours allow interested audiences to explore these topics in a safe, informative environment while providing context for those viewers to see current events in a new light. Sometimes knowing our history can help inform our futures, and in this way, museum professionals who offer such tours and programs at their respective institutions are participating in their own forms of advocacy. This openness and willingness to discuss difficult and sometimes polarizing subjects aids in gaining millennial respect and in positioning those museums as relevant to a millennial audience.

Textbox 4.2

"We have seen an overwhelmingly positive response from the millennial generation in regard to this type of programming . . . we are proud that we have told and continue to tell a balanced story." —Matt Davis, Director of Historic Houses, Georgia College

---

Relevance is also often synonymous with nostalgia for a millennial audience. For most millennials, the 1980s and 1990s and their associated trends made up the bulk of their collective childhoods. Like all generations, they usually remember childhood with a fondness characterized by a lack of responsibility, anxiety, or fear. These negative emotions are more closely associated with adulthood and the trials and tribulations it brings to people trying to navigate life in their twenties and thirties. Nostalgic activities provide an escape from the difficulties of adulthood, and based on many of the numbers being purported by news and research organizations, millennials need an escape. As discussed in the first chapter, many millennials are in massive debt due to a higher education system that is failing them, while others are unable to provide for themselves due to the lack of good paying jobs available to them as an entry-level worker. This perfect storm of high debt and the lack of sufficient employment provides the basis for the near constant fear of failure and heightened sense of anxiety many millennials feel. It is no wonder millennials value mentally escaping to the safety of childhood. Fellow millennial Michaela Francis identifies with these struggles and uses museums as an escape. She says museums bring her joy, and she goes to them whenever she can. [4] Many millennials share her feelings.

Textbox 4.3

"Museums bring me such joy." —Michaela Francis, 25

Author Tina Wells provides the best summation of the millennial experience and attitude in her work *Chasing Youth Culture and Getting It Right*. She states:

> It seems as though people are in an almost permanent state of reflection these days. Whether they're thinking back to times that were more financially secure or less stressful (or a little of both), we're entering a period during which people want to reminisce. Can you blame them? It's only human nature to focus on a time or place that made you feel safe and comfortable. It's called nostalgia.[5]

The culture in which these millennials grew up offers many avenues for crafting programming based on nostalgic elements, and based on the rise in anxiety among millennials and the success of marketing among nostalgic brands, this is a good route to take. Disney and all of its associated characters are a prime example of a nostalgic company. Most girls in the millennial generation grew up with Disney characters, and as a result, dressed up as a princess or read the associated Little Golden Books. The most popular events at my museum involve character appearances by Mary Poppins, Professor

Trelawney, and Alice in Wonderland because they bring back that sense of wonder and safety girls in this generation experienced through the books and movies that marked their childhood experiences. Men also attend our literary events, which one person stated reminded him of when he fell in love with books as a child. He was attending a Poe reading and it was nostalgic for him because it reminded him of reading Poe's works in school, and how those works helped mold his interests.

Perhaps the question here is how museum professionals can incorporate a love of nostalgic characters into serious, educational programming. It can be done; the secret lies in understanding the mission of your facility and carefully choosing characters which fit in to that mission. My museum is Victorian, so we stick with characters from stories written in the nineteenth century or those which embody attitudes of the nineteenth century. Our mission statement allows us to extend into the early twentieth century as well, so we recently added the Mary Poppins programming which has worked well. Literary evenings, such as readings or plays, are relatively easy events to put on and to customize to your museum's mission. They also provide an educational component that is usually vital to a museum's mission.

Such events are but one example of how museum professionals can capitalize on this need for nostalgia to attract a millennial audience. Offering guests the chance to dress up is always a popular option, especially with the ladies who recall a time as little girls when they played dress up, either themselves or with dolls. Such events also provide an added sense of escapism by

---

Textbox 4.4

CREATE OPPORTUNITIES FOR NOSTALGIA

Millennials enjoy escaping from the trials and tribulations of life by trying out different personas for small amounts of time. Many respond well to events which allow them to reminisce about their childhood. Give them an opportunity to dress up and relax by providing participatory experiences. Incorporate your mission, collection, or related themes to keep it current and relevant. Costumes, food, and fun are a recipe for success for millennial engagement.

allowing participants to become someone else for an afternoon, perhaps as a guest at tea or character in a murder mystery. Educational components can always be added to these types of events, as is evidenced at Clouds Hill Museum in Warwick, Rhode Island. The volunteer-run organization puts on various types of educational programming throughout the year that appeal to a millennial audience. The most fitting example of a relevant program for millennials they have offered is a *Downton Abbey*–themed tea titled In the Style of *Downton Abbey*.[6] While *Downton Abbey* itself is not something that the attendees would have watched as children, the series does provide an opportunity to wax nostalgic about tea times with Grandma as a child. It is most appealing because attendees were also encouraged to dress in the style of the show, which provided a sense of escape from reality and all the negative aspects of adult life. To make this event fit in with the museum's mission, attendees were also given access to the textile exhibit that was running simultaneously and highlighted the textile industry in Rhode Island.[7] The event was well attended by young people, most of whom were delighted to have a chance to dress the part and enjoy the afternoon with friends and family.

Events like these can be duplicated in various formats and themes, but all share the common thread of using nostalgia as a way in to the hearts and minds of the millennial generation. Millennials see relevance as a dichotomous concept defined by childhood loves and current fears, times of safety and times of scarcity, and being young and accepted and being an adult and fighting for rights. In order for a museum to be relevant, museum staff should recognize the need for social awareness and advocacy as well as the need to provide a safe, nostalgic environment for a millennial audience.

STAYING ON MISSION

It is easy to think the best way to attract a millennial audience is to create a beer fest with kegs, a live punk band, and food trucks. I am not suggesting there is not a market for that, but it likely isn't the kind of repeat visitor you want to attract. They will come for the beer, the music, and the food, but will they ever return for a tour or an educational program? The programs you choose to offer send a clear message to your intended audience about what your museum values. If I were to see the aforementioned event advertised and there was not an educational component, I would assume the museum was simply out to turn a profit. This is not the message you want to send to serious visitors who may become volunteers, museum members, or donors. This is why it is vital, and I mean absolutely necessary, that every event you serve up to the public, for millennials or otherwise, aligns with the mission of your facility. We all need to bring in funds to survive, but ensuring our collective integrity as respected places of knowledge is the most vital mission of all.

If you are struggling to determine if your event idea is in alignment with your museum's mission, ask yourself these questions:

- What are the core values of my facility? Are those values reflected in the event description and marketing plans?
- Will offering this event simply expand my audience, or will it also expose that audience to the museum's values?
- What will visitors take away from the experience? Will they walk away with an accurate idea of who we are, what we do, and what is important to us?

I call these questions a "Value Check System." If you are unable to clearly decide if an event is reflecting the values you want the community to associate with your facility, then push that event to the side. No amount of money is worth compromising the clear message you send to your audience of who you are and what you value.

So, how does this compute to attracting a millennial audience? If there is one thing millennials value, it is honesty. Above all else, millennials appreciate clarity of purpose and honest marketing of that purpose, which is one of the many reasons they often support avenues for social advocacy. Most people, millennials included, visit museums with the hope of walking out of them with more knowledge than they walked in with; this means that providing mission-driven programming will allow for millennials to always walk away with a better understanding of the values of the facility and how they fit into supporting those values.

One of the most relevant exhibits I have seen to date was a traveling Smithsonian exhibit called the Art of Video Games. I happened to see it locally at the Chrysler Museum of Art in Norfolk, Virginia, but it traveled across the country and was viewed, or rather experienced, by thousands of patrons. It would be difficult to see how this could not attract a millennial audience. The exhibit was interactive, educational, and simultaneously nostalgic and current. I can honestly say this is one of the most well-attended exhibits I have personally seen. On the day I saw the exhibit, there were more twenty- and thirty-year-old men in the room than I had seen in a month's time at my museum. The turnout was incredible, and the staff of the Chrysler Museum of Art graciously shared their visitation numbers with me to prove it. Over a three-month period, the museum was visited by over 57,000 people, most of which likely experienced the exhibit.[8] The Chrysler Museum of Art is but one example of many museums who housed this exhibit while it toured and experienced an overwhelmingly positive response. The question is: why?

The Art of Video Games exhibit seamlessly intertwined the millennial generation's love for nostalgia, technology, and entertainment with the museum's mission to provide access to art and educational opportunities. The exhibit highlighted the museum's mission to educate by allowing patrons to see, perhaps for the first time, the video game as an art form. The exhibit consisted of vintage game consoles, some of which could be played, and the Chrysler Museum of Art's exhibit ended with an arcade of nostalgic games from the millennial childhood provided by a local business.[9] It discussed the transformation of computer graphics over time and digital media as a form of art. This exhibit was meant to work from its inception, since its curator took the time to poll perspective visitors and their thoughts on which games should be included while designing the exhibit. This is a great example of audience-sourced feedback that significantly aided in the success of the overall project. Museum professionals should never underestimate the validity of audience feedback at any stage in the event planning process. For this exhibit, the audience engagement component really set it apart from other exhibits by making it personal and relevant.

Textbox 4.5

"As a Museum Educator, I felt it was extremely valuable to bring an exhibition like The Art of Video Games to the Chrysler Museum of Art. We saw many families visiting the exhibition because the parents would remember these games from their childhood, while their children would be interested in the newer gaming systems they currently use . . . the combination of nostalgia and interactivity allowed the community to experience art like they never had before." —Meagan Douglas, Museum Educator for Wonder Studio and Family Experiences, Chrysler Museum of Art

The Art of Video Games exhibit was viewed at museums in D.C., Florida, Washington, Arizona, New York, Ohio, Michigan, Tennessee, and Virginia between 2012 and 2016.[10] I attended in 2015, and to this day, it remains in my mind the foremost example of providing successful avenues for millennial engagement in a museum setting. The exhibit provided a sense of escapism for a millennial audience, which contributed to its popularity. It was an unforgettable experience, and many millennials enjoyed being able to take on their childhood persona for a small amount of time while learning about the video game as an art form.

The Mystic Seaport Museum recently offered a program that worked very well for their facility and stayed on mission while providing relevant, immersing experiences for a millennial audience. The event was a series called Seaport After Seven and featured a nightlife experience focused around an exhibit at the museum. Arlene Marcionette, the Public Programs Project Manager, described the series as "edgier, louder, highly social, and with a low price point," making it enticing to a millennial audience.[11] The event, or experience rather, offered focused exhibition access and educational components in addition to themed games, food, a DJ, and a cash bar. She noted the most successful of the series had been a Viking Beer Garden night that featured a Vikings exhibit which incorporated items from the seventh century that had never left the original country of Sweden prior to this exhibit.[12] The museum offered Viking-inspired foods and lawn games in addition to renegade tours provided by Museum Hack.[13] Between the addition of Museum Hack, the use of a very popular theme in current culture, and after-hours access, this event was set up to succeed. Arlene notes they have seen clear and steady growth, with their numbers increasing from 75 people for the first event to 350 for the last event in the series.[14] They used social media for marketing and did a few radio advertisements, but other than that, the experience marketed itself. They also employed a creative marketing tool by advertising that the first 50 people to arrive in Viking costume would receive an extra ticket.[15] This is sure to be an event they will repeat with the upcoming exhibits being featured. It is, as we can see, possible to create fun experiences while staying on mission and promoting your facility's collection. For more information, please see textbox 4.6.

> **Textbox 4.6**
>
> **Event Highlight:** *Seaport After Seven: Viking Beer Garden*
>
> **Facility:** Mystic Seaport Museum
>
> **Location:** Mystic, Connecticut
>
> **Budget:** >$300,000 (Mid-sized museum)
>
> **Event Description:** "Seaport After Seven returns—and we're going big to kick off the season!
>
> Celebrate warmer weather and two brand new exhibitions when the 21+ party series returns on Saturday, May 19, with the **Viking Beer Garden**. Enjoy outdoor breezes, Swedish meatballs, a variety of beers, and mead by Groennfell Meadery on the giant wraparound deck of the Thompson Exhibition Building. For one night only, **Museum Hack** will lead renegade tours of not one, but two exhibitions: The Vikings Begin and Science, Myth, and Mystery: The Vinland Map Saga. **DJ Lion King** will provide beats while you brush up on your Kubb skills (AKA Viking chess on the lawn) and step aboard an authentic Viking long ship, the *Draken Harald Hårfagre*. Bring your friends, make some new ones, and have a truly radical night at the Museum!
>
> The first 50 people to arrive in Viking-inspired attire will receive an extra drink ticket!
>
> This is a 21+ event. Admission includes small plates, one drink ticket for beer or wine, exclusive exhibition access and tours, and DJ set. A cash bar with beer, wine and mead will be available."
> (Pulled directly from https://www.mysticseaport.org/event/seaport-after -seven-viking-beer-garden/)
>
> **Attendance:** 350
>
> **Primary Ways Marketed:** Social media platforms (boosted posts)
>
> **Public Programs Project Manager's Take:** The *Seaport After Seven* series "gave the feel of an edgier, louder, highly social environment with a

low price point . . . we have seen clear and steady growth with the event series." —Arlene Marcionette, Public Programs Project Manager

Why It Works: This event offered an affordable ticket price of around $20, which made it a low-cost opportunity for millennials to experience art in a fun atmosphere. Games, food, and the environment itself were themed around a special exhibit. The evenings were interactive, educational, and entertaining. Tours were given by known millennial engagement team *Museum Hack*, which aided in the laid-back and informal feel of the evening. The event felt relevant to a millennial audience, in part, because the unofficial millennial advisory board was used to help plan this event series. Having an insider from the millennial world is a very helpful way to ensure the programming you create is relevant to this audience.

Arlene was the only person I spoke with who readily offered an example of a program that is still a work in progress. Her willingness to share the struggle of crafting a relevant program for millennials will hopefully provide insight for museum professionals regarding how it is possible to over plan, or place too much emphasis on a theme thought to be popular with millennials. The event she is hoping to revamp was a trial run at a trivia night. The museum partnered with a local group who created themed trivia evenings centered around special exhibits hosted by the museum. Arlene tried two trivia nights, and had high hopes for success for each, but felt disheartened when the second in the series did not result in more attendance than the first, but in less. Each trivia evening included snacks, a cash bar, and trivia themed around an exhibit. The trivia was supposed to complement the exhibits and vice versa, since those who viewed the exhibit and then attended the trivia evening would likely have an advantage.[16] The first evening seemed promising, bringing out close to forty individuals. The turnout for the second trivia night, though, left Arlene wondering where they went wrong. The second evening was theoretically supposed to bring in a larger crowd than the first because it was Viking-themed and should have brought a return audience, but only twenty people came out for the event. Arlene and her staff were, understandably, disappointed.[17]

There were two major differences between the first and second evening, though, that likely caused the confusing result of decreased attendance: type of food and price point. The first event featured typical bar snacks, a cash bar, and trivia, but was free to attend. The second event featured Viking-themed foods, a cash bar, and trivia, but at a price point of $25 per person.[18] While millennials are willing to pay for unique experiences that excite them, the Viking-themed menu likely proved to be a point of contention when deciding to attend the event. On a superficial level, the themed food should draw in a millennial audience for this event; however, the food itself, while authentic, proved less appetizing than standard bar fare at that price point. Trivia nights are a popular activity for millennials, and with so many local bars, coffee shops, and other venues offering them regularly and cheaply, it is easy to think the best way to stand out from the crowd is to go over-the-top with things like themed food and drinks; but the truth is, millennials enjoy the lower price point with the basic bar food. The themed food, when weighed against a higher price, simply did not hold up. Arlene recognized this was likely the place where they went awry. They over-planned and tried too hard to be unique in their offerings. All museum professionals should pay attention to Arlene's reaction to this undesired result; she said she refused to give up hope. She and her team are working together, going back to the drawing board, using their millennial advisory group, and taking everything they have learned to regroup and try the event again.[19] This is the exact attitude museum professionals need to have when they feel they have missed the mark with the millennial demographic; try and try again.

PRACTICAL APPLICATIONS

The millennial subgroups, on the whole, experience relevance similarly. They all perceive value in museums through the experiences they have with them, whether from a nostalgic or advocacy standpoint. In order to remain relevant to all of these subgroups, museum professionals should strive to make their facility a community cornerstone above all else; they need to create a sense of comfort and hominess at their facilities. Doing so will ensure that millennials of all backgrounds, and those of other generations for that matter, will frequent their institution.

This can take many forms, but one of the best examples I have seen comes from a relatively new museum called the Mosaic Templars Cultural Center in

Little Rock, Arkansas. The focus of this facility is African American heritage; the history of African Americans, their contributions to the past, and their place in the future. Christina Shutt, the director of the facility, provided valuable insight into how their facility is literally a gathering place for those in the community and the ways in which they use their platform and access to engage those of all economic levels in their local vicinity. Recently, they partnered with their local chamber to aid them in their economic development week. The chamber provided refreshments and the museum was given a platform to show what they can provide for the community while incorporating an educational component in the form of a 1900s living history demonstration.[20] The chamber reported this was the most well attended event they had seen in recent years, and Christina says it will continue to be on their calendar each year.[21] This community outreach allowed for the museum to act as a catalyst for change while also being a beacon for communal gatherings.

The Mosaic Templars Cultural Center also engages with the community by filling their educational needs and offering classes for local artisans. Christina described an initiative called Arkansas Made, Black Crafted which is about two years old. It allows the museum staff to connect with African American makers in the community crafting their own jewelry, scarves, lotions, soaps, and other wares.[22] These items are then taken in on consignment and sold in the gift shop. In order to promote good business practice and ethics, the museum offers small business classes for these individuals and others in conjunction with the Economic Development Commission. Christina pointed out that the need for this was great because these makers, the majority of which are millennials, have worthwhile and creative ideas but little practical business experience.[23] These classes and the platform the museum offers by selling their items in the shop give them an advantage in becoming successful entrepreneurs they likely would not have otherwise. This facility plays an invaluable role in the community by investing in the future of these millennials; I suspect they will continue to thrive for many years to come as a direct result.

The Mosaic Templars Cultural Center also offered an exhibit in the summer of 2018 that promoted relevancy from a practical standpoint. The exhibit, titled Don't Touch my Crown, looked at the history and culture of African American beauty. It focused specifically on hair, and the staff created programming to accompany this theme.[24] Director Christina Shutt discussed the exhibit at length, stating that among the programs they offered were a Hair

---

Textbox 4.7

ENGAGE YOUR COMMUNITY

Want to be part of your community, but classes and partnerships are not working for you? Try another route by working to diversify your audience. Take your show on the road! Set up booths at local festivals and farmer's markets. Millennials love organic foods and locally grown produce, so you are likely to find them in these places. Bring along any millennial volunteers or employees at your disposal, so they can tell other millennials firsthand what makes your museum relevant to them. Millennial parents are also reachable through the Girl Scouts and Boy Scouts. They often host fairs for nonprofits to attend; check their calendar, bring snazzy prizes, and network. You can do this!

Show and themed lectures. She commented that the offerings created a high turnout among a millennial audience who found value in the programming and resonated with the subject matter.[25] What caught my attention was a lecture they offered that was given by a scientist who specialized in scalp and hair care as part of a lunchtime series.[26] This individual gave a lecture on how best to care for one's hair and scalp and it was very well-attended by a millennial audience. This program was perceived as relevant by this demographic because it served a practical purpose while incorporating entertainment, history, and art. In a two-month period, Christina reports visitation in the tens of thousands.[27] Museum professionals should try to determine the needs of their communities and capitalize on those needs by offering relevant programming like the Mosaic Templars Cultural Center. Such efforts will undoubtedly prove fruitful in attracting an engaged millennial audience.

Keep in mind that millennial parents are interested not only in what is relevant to them, but what is relevant to their children, as well. This means that museum professionals are tasked with providing activities that will please both the parent and the child. One suggestion for making relevant and entertaining programming for all ages to enjoy is to go back to the basics. Try incorporating classic programming into your museum's calendar and gauge the reaction. This can mean anything from an ice cream social to games on your front lawn. One of the reasons museum professionals see a surge in attendance among millennial families at music festivals and outdoor movie screenings is not the beer that is served or the music or movie that is played, it is that the museum is offering a place for the child and adult to spend an afternoon or evening together and reconnect despite their varied interests. Most of these festivals and such also have bounce houses and sweet treats for the little ones, and millennial parents really value events that allow for the whole family to attend and enjoy themselves.

You might be wondering how this is any different than any other generation. In truth, it really isn't; however, I would argue millennial parents place an almost greater emphasis on family time because of their concern over a lack of time and resources. Authors Jeff Fromm and Melissa Vidler support this notion, stating "higher value placed on time means that new moms are more interested in creating experiences for their children and families that are worthwhile and a good use of their time."[28] They go on to suggest that their research has found that "millennial parents are more likely to make purchase decisions based on price, [but] they are still willing to dish out big bucks for products that have an impact on their family"[29] This means your staff should not be afraid to try new types of programming with a high price tag simply because millennials generally do not have loads of disposable income; rather, you should take the leap of faith to craft valuable programming with a reasonable price point and use your marketing department to create campaigns geared at promoting the event as an experience that will be valuable for the whole family. Through this approach, your facility may become a preferred place for engagement for both millennial parents and their children.

In summation, millennials find museums most relevant when their programs reflect their values, their collective need for nostalgia and escapism, and promote diversity and inclusion. Millennials from all subgroups appreciate programming that is perceived as valuable, both in terms of time and resources spent. Millennial parents are particularly concerned with time and cost but will attend events and become loyal brand ambassadors when a museum's staff succeeds in convincing them of the value of their facility's programming and their own relevancy. Museums are uniquely positioned to provide these experiences through an educational and welcoming atmosphere. Fellow museum professionals, it is time to take up the challenge to become relevant to the millennial audience by reevaluating your current offerings and adjusting them to meet the needs of this eager patron generation.

NOTES

1. "The Three Keys to Ongoing Millennial Engagement for Cultural Organizations—Colleen Dilenschneider," https://www.colleendilen.com/2018/07/11/three-keys-ongoing-millennial-engagement-cultural-organizations/ (accessed August 20, 2018).

2. Matt Davis (Director of Historic Houses, Georgia College) in discussion with the author, July 2018. For more information on Georgia's Old Governor's Mansion, please visit their website at http://www.gcsu.edu/mansion.

3. "Tour the Mansion—Georgia's Old Governor's Mansion—Georgia College," http://www.gcsu.edu/mansion/tours (accessed August 27, 2018).

4. Michaela Francis (Millennial) in discussion with the author, June 2018.

5. Wells, *Chasing Youth Culture and Getting It Right*, 104.

6. "Calendar," http://www.cloudshill.org/calendar.html (accessed June 30, 3018). For more information on Clouds Hill Victorian House Museum, please visit their website at http://www.cloudshill.org.

7. "Calendar," http://www.cloudshill.org/calendar.html (accessed June 30, 3018).

8. The museum does not keep visitation numbers for specific exhibits, but rather foot traffic for the museum as a whole. They did note, though, that their visual assessment of the exhibit itself suggests it was one of the most well-attended they had seen in years. These numbers were provided by email from Meagan Douglas, Museum Educator for Wonder Studio and Family Experiences at the Chrysler Museum of Art, on August 14, 2018.

9. "Exhibitions at the Chrysler Museum of Art—Chrysler Museum of Art," http://www.chrysler.org/exhibitions/the-art-of-video-games/ (accessed August 27, 2018).

10. "The Art of Video Games: Smithsonian American Art Museum," https://americanart.si.edu/exhibitions/games (accessed July 15, 2018).

11. Arlene Marcionette (Public Programs Project Manager, Mystic Seaport Museum) in discussion with the author, August 2018.

12. Arlene Marcionette (Public Programs Project Manager, Mystic Seaport Museum) in discussion with the author, August 2018.

13. "Seaport After Seven: Viking Beer Garden—Mystic Seaport," https://www.mysticseaport.org/event/seaport-after-seven-viking-beer-garden/ (accessed August 1, 2018).

14. Arlene Marcionette (Public Programs Project Manager, Mystic Seaport Museum) in discussion with the author, August 2018.

15. "Seaport After Seven: Viking Beer Garden—Mystic Seaport," https://www.mysticseaport.org/event/seaport-after-seven-viking-beer-garden/ (accessed August 1, 2018).

16. Arlene Marcionette (Public Programs Project Manager, Mystic Seaport Museum) in discussion with the author, August 2018.

17. Arlene Marcionette (Public Programs Project Manager, Mystic Seaport Museum) in discussion with the author, August 2018.

18. Arlene Marcionette (Public Programs Project Manager, Mystic Seaport Museum) in discussion with the author, August 2018.

19. Arlene Marcionette (Public Programs Project Manager, Mystic Seaport Museum) in discussion with the author, August 2018.

20. Christina Shutt (Director Mosaic Templars Cultural Association) in discussion with the author, August 2018. For more information about the Mosaic Templars Cultural Association, please visit their website at http://www.mosaictemplarscenter.org.

21. Christina Shutt (Director Mosaic Templars Cultural Association) in discussion with the author, August 2018.

22. "Store," http://www.mosaictemplarscenter.com/store (accessed August 20, 2018).

23. Christina Shutt (Director Mosaic Templars Cultural Association) in discussion with the author, August 2018.

24. "Don't Touch My Crown," http://www.mosaictemplarscenter.com/Exhibits/dont-touch-my-crown (accessed August 27, 2018).

25. Christina Shutt (Director Mosaic Templars Cultural Association) in discussion with the author, August 2018.

26. "Hair+ Lunch & Learn Series." https://www.facebook.com/events/564999170 566656/ (accessed August 27, 2018).

27. Christina Shutt (Director Mosaic Templars Cultural Association) in discussion with the author, August 2018.

28. Fromm and Vidler, *Millennials with Kids*, 56.

29. Fromm and Vidler, *Millennials with Kids*, 48.

A: "Accessibility"

THIS chapter seeks to position accessibility as a key factor in the millennial decision to patronize museums and cultural institutions. First, this chapter will explain what accessibility means for millennials in a museum context by defining the term and highlighting areas of importance for a millennial audience. Then, this chapter will discuss why accessibility is a key factor. Lastly, this chapter will provide examples of programs that embody accessibility that have proven successful at various museums. This discussion will include references to millennial subgroups and how the idea of accessibility differs for each group. By the end of this chapter, readers should be able to define accessibility from a millennial standpoint, understand why accessibility is a key factor in the decision process for millennials to visit museums, and recognize the differences in the applications of the idea of accessibility for each millennial subgroup.

DEFINING ACCESSIBILITY

Much like the concept of relevance, accessibility is a term that can contain multiple meanings and applications. According to the American Alliance of Museums (AAM), accessibility can be defined as "giving equitable access to everyone along the continuum of human ability and experience."[1] Accessibility "encompasses the broader meanings of compliance and refers to how organizations make space for the characteristics that each person brings."[2] In the museum world, accessibility can take the form of accommodations for physical and intellectual disabilities, perceived ease of locating and obtaining physical access to the facility itself, or providing a facility that is welcoming to individuals of all ages and backgrounds. For millennials, like most other generations, all of these factors play an important role in deciding whether or not to patronize your facility.

Millennials have grown up in and continue to live in a world that tells them they can have what they want when they want it. Technology makes it possible for millennials to connect in real-time with area businesses through their websites, social media, and other avenues. Many online retailers capitalize on this millennial demand by making purchasing easier, such as the Amazon one-click option to buy items, or by offering instant methods of communication, such as the messenger component on social media programs. This idea extends into their expectations of the world of museums and cultural institutions. Millennials expect to have access to new and favorite places alike, and to have that access on their own time and terms. This means that millennials favor businesses that have quick and effective response rates to online communication, provide clear and easily understood information about their pricing and operating hours on an online platform, and make efforts to maintain an active online presence. Harkening back to their fear of missing out, millennials do not want to waste time searching for the best ways to visit your facility; they want the information available at their fingertips and accessible at a moment's notice. This can be a challenge for many cultural institutions with small staff sizes and budgets; nonetheless it is an expectation that millennials possess for all museums, big and small. Excuses are not accepted by the millennial audience; frequent, open, and easy communication is a basic expectation.

Like other generations, millennials also expect to be able to literally access your physical facility. One of the most frustrating things that can happen to any museum visitor is to not be able to locate the museum based on given directions, or for there to be a lack of signage once a visitor is there, making it difficult to find the entrance to the facility. Again, millennials expect ease of access. This is not a generational expectation as much as a general one. Visitors want to feel empowered when visiting your site, which means they want to know they have the correct information and tools to have a pleasurable museum experience. Clear signage, explicit driving directions, and a friendly front-door staff member are all integral components in ensuring these expectations are met.

In an interview conducted with fellow millennial and museum enthusiast Joshua Weinstein, he described a situation to me in which he felt very uncomfortable and unwelcome, mainly due to a lack of signage and lack of clear communication from key staff members.[3] Joshua was visiting an institution in Philadelphia while in the city and was interested in seeing a particular exhibit they had on display. When he entered the museum, there was a front desk to go to for check-in and pay admission. There was not any signage, but because he had worked in a museum with a similar layout, he deduced that this was the entry point and made his way to the desk. The front desk staff member did not give him explicit instructions regarding entering the exhibit space, so he had to decide which of the two doorways to enter through: the one on the entire other end of the room or the one nearest the desk. He chose to head for the doorway closest to the desk. The desk attendant did not say anything to him, so he assumed he could use this doorway. Once inside, he was met by a gallery attendant, or security guard, who had been manning the room. Joshua began to look at the exhibit and was then stopped by this museum attendant and instructed that he had come in the wrong door and the exhibit actually began at the other end where the farthest doorway was located. Joshua thanked him and explained that he was not told, but that it did not matter to him and he would view the exhibit from back to front since it was not in any particular order. The attendant was insistent that Josh exit the doorway and begin at the "beginning." Joshua ignored him, quickly rushed through the exhibit, and left the museum feeling unwelcome and angry.[4] This museum's staff did a poor job of being accessible on many fronts, and Joshua has not returned since.

In this example, how could this have been avoided? If this was your museum, what changes could have been instituted to ensure this did not happen in the first place? Here are a few ideas:

- Place clear signage at all entry and exit points to the facility and to individual exhibits on display
- Train front desk or entryway staff to instruct visitors on the layout of the facility as they enter
- Conduct staff meetings to ensure all staff who interact with guests are effectively communicating and reinforcing the same information

- Remind staff that it is not their job to tell people how to experience the museum, just to give them access to the experience

The last bullet was the sticking point for Joshua. He said he had dealt with rude museum attendants before, but he could not abide someone attempting to instruct him on how to experience art.[5] Like most millennials, Joshua wished to have the experience in his own way and without being told what he was supposed to think or feel. This museum attendant robbed him of this experience, and ultimately made him feel so unwelcome that he left the facility. If he was this forthcoming with his story to me, he has probably told it many times to his friends and family. This negative review by word of mouth could prove detrimental for many museums, and it is completely avoidable. All it requires is forethought, training, and good signage.

Textbox 5.1

LISTEN TO THEIR FEEDBACK

One of the most difficult issues within any career is receiving negative feedback. In the museum world, this reaction could literally manifest itself in a lack of attendance or a harsh online review. It is vital for your staff to learn from these instances and choose to grow from them. Put effort into training your staff, creating user-friendly signage, and making sure all visitor interactions with your staff are positive. This will make your institution truly accessible.

It is also imperative to include operating hours as part of this discussion of accessibility. In previous chapters, we have discussed that while it is difficult to most millennials to acquire full-time work with benefits, that does not mean they do not work. Actually, the contrary is true. Millennials often work multiple jobs to make ends meet, and this means the typical nine-to-five workday is slowly disappearing from the millennial workplace landscape. As a result, millennial leisure time is changing as well. If you want millennials to frequent your institution, you must do your best to offer programs and entry to the facility at times other than the standard operating hours. This means offering after-hours programs, early morning entry for those with children, and expanding general operating hours as you are able. According to Colleen Dilenschneider, "Schedule is the single biggest factor contributing to visitation."[6] In other words, if you create amazing programs and offer stellar exhibits, that is great; but if you do not create opportunities for accessibility that go beyond your regular operating hours, you may miss out on millennial attendance and engagement entirely. This is another area in which having millennial input is vital for success. Like with other groups mentioned in previous chapters, try creating a millennial advisory board, ask your millennial volunteers or staff members, or put the question to the public on your social media page: what time of day would you attend a program? It seems simple, but this small change can help you and your staff avoid working tirelessly on an event geared toward millennials only to have no millennials show up due to the time of day. It is vital to keep this in mind when thinking about accessibility and your museum or cultural institution.

As should be expected, accessibility is important to millennials in terms of creating a welcoming environment that allows for diversity to shine. We have previously discussed that millennials value diversity in part because they are the most accepting and ethnically diverse generation to date. The Pew Research Center also reports that millennials "are more receptive to immigrants . . . nearly 58% say immigrants strengthen the country."[7] This means millennials expect their places of recreation to reflect those values and actively seek out ways in which to engage new and diverse audiences. Last chapter we discussed the importance of millennials seeing themselves reflected in marketing efforts. This ties into the concept of accessibility because these marketing campaigns have the capacity to make these individuals feel welcome at the facility. Your facility would be remiss in discounting the level of importance millennials place on being surrounded by people who think and look differently than them. Millennials celebrate that they live in a diverse world and expect their visits to museums and cultural institutions to value and reflect this concept.

Lastly, accessibility can be defined in terms of accommodating physical and intellectual disabilities. Communication of the limitations of the facility and its accommodations are key in creating and maintaining the trust of the museum audience in general. This is of the utmost importance to millennials, who as we have mentioned previously, value honesty and direct communication very highly. ADA compliance is something some entities,

FIGURE 5.1
Confusion at the Museum
Created for Publication by Morven Moeller, 2018

such as historic house museums, are not necessarily required to observe. For entities like historic house museums, it is imperative that staff members are educated, open, and honest about the physical limitations of the buildings. Post somewhere on your website and social media pages that the facility is not handicap-accessible, has spiral staircases, or other issues that will make it impossible for individuals with physical disabilities to be accommodated. For those with intellectual disabilities, be forthcoming about how tours or programs can be accommodated to the needs of those individuals. If the museum offers special days, hours, or programs specifically for those with special needs, be sure to point that out to inquirers. The best way to create an accessible atmosphere is to be honest about the limitations of your facility. Even if some individuals cannot be accommodated, by being honest and open with these individuals, you are protecting your brand recognition and securing the integrity of your facility.

ACCESSIBILITY AND MILLENNIAL EXPECTATIONS

In a blog post from 2015, museum professional Loretta Mordi highlights the areas in which museum professionals from around the world should be focusing when thinking about making changes toward a more inclusive environment.[8] Mordi mentions physical changes to the facility, such as signage, ramps, and labels on exhibit materials, as well as web accessibility.[9] While museum leadership is well aware of the ADA requirements their respective facilities must meet and why those accommodations are necessary for guests with disabilities, web accessibility is something that often falls by the wayside. Mordi does well to highlight it here, since in this discussion, it should be obvious that web connectivity and accessibility is of paramount importance to the millennial generation. We already know millennials are the most connected generation to date, since they literally grew up alongside the rise of technology and the internet. Because millennials expect technology and its accessibility to grow as they have grown, they expect constant and honest communication and easy accessibility to the institutions they patronize; museums and cultural institutions fall under this umbrella.

For millennials, accessibility is a key factor in the decision to visit museums and cultural institutions because it aligns with their collective value system. Millennials view accessibility as synonymous with ideas like inclusion, honesty, and diversity. These are values associated with the generation as a whole that have been well documented in findings by researchers, many of which we have previously discussed. Millennials are more apt to respect and patronize those businesses and institutions which subscribe to these same ideals. Museums and cultural institutions, with their varying scopes and sizes, are positioned to embody these values in ways that are unique to their facilities. Millennials recognize and appreciate those efforts.

Perhaps the even greater expectation millennials have about accessibility and museums is frequent, helpful communication. Millennials live in a fast-paced world with limited time and funds available for visiting museums and cultural institutions. If your museum has managed to attract the attention of a millennial audience, one of the biggest culprits of not seeing return visitation could be that your facility inadvertently possesses impediments to easy access. If someone emails or messages your facility on a social media platform and staff do not respond for two or three days, this sends the message to the millennial inquirer that their time and interest are not valued by the facility. Millennials have a need to be needed, and this perceived slight is not going to entice them to continue reaching out to your museum. In fact, maintaining acceptable levels of response time can be a make-or-break tool for your facility. When you respond to inquiries in a timely manner, say within an hour on a messaging platform, you send the message to the individual that you value their time and are genuinely interested in their concerns. If your museum has a small staff and is not able to maintain frequent availability on social media platforms, it is imperative for your facility to institute regular hours for online communication. This can mean using an "away" message on Facebook to send automatically when someone messages outside of your online response hours. Within the message, you should state when they can expect to hear back from you. This will maintain the expected level of accessibility while ensuring your staff is able to perform all of its assigned duties and avoid burnout.

In her presidential address at the 2010 annual meeting of the National Council on Public History, Marianne Babel described the expectations of a museum visitor as wanting their museum experience to "be communicated in ways personally relevant, memorable, meaningful, emotional, sensory, and increasingly, experiential."[10] Her words embody the feelings of the millennial audience, with whom museum professionals must actively communicate in new and relevant ways. Accessibility plays a key role in delivering these relevant messages to this audience. The two concepts work hand in hand;

Textbox 5.2

PRO-TIP: AWAY MESSAGES
MAINTAIN PERCEIVED ACCESSIBILITY

Does your facility have limited staff, or share the responsibilities of posting to social media platforms? Work smarter, not harder, while ensuring you maintain your brand identity by utilizing tools like the Facebook Messenger "Away" message feature. This feature allows you to personalize a message to the sender wherein you can state that you are delighted they messaged the facility, value their time, and will return their inquiry in a timely manner. Be sure to state a specific time frame in which they can expect to hear from you to ensure their expectations are set to a reasonable level. This will help you avoid any negative feedback from a millennial audience, who value entities who place value on their time and interactions.

without accessible information and physical structure, the relevance of a museum's programming and mission statement do not matter. If you build it, millennials will only come if they know how to get there, with whom to communicate, and through which channels. The best way to ensure your communication methods are proving effective is to meet millennials where they are, which generally means on a virtual level. Create social media accounts that millennials frequently use, such as Instagram, and maintain an active and constant presence on those sites. If you have accounts on half a dozen social media accounts, but only post once weekly and sporadically answer messages from millennial users, then you are only hurting your museum and its perceived image. Social media can be used for good, but only if used properly and regularly. If you work for a small institution and cannot manage to actively communicate on multiple platforms, pick one and be as accessible on that platform as possible. As you grow your user base and bring in more of a millennial audience, you can expand your social media usage to other platforms. Instagram and Facebook are your best bets if you have limited personnel, but keep in mind other platforms like Twitter, Pinterest, and YouTube can prove useful as well. It is okay to start small, but do it well.

Millennials will appreciate your authenticity and your ability to remain accessible through constant communication on online platforms.

PRACTICAL APPLICATIONS

There are basic foundational ideas regarding accessibility that millennials of all subgroups share. First and foremost, millennials expect clear and constant communication with your facility. This means online, in print, and in person. Signage at the physical facility should be clear, your social media campaigns and conversations should have a high degree of synergy, and your staff should be well-trained and able to answer basic questions about accessibility. Single millennials, millennials in relationships, and millennial parents value all of these aspects.

The subgroup which may expect more accommodations than the others is the millennial parent group. Whenever any parent chooses to visit a museum or cultural site, they have basic expectations about the safety of the facility and its degree of child-friendliness. Your staff should be on the same page when addressing these concerns, providing accurate information about realistic expectations for children visiting the facility. There is nothing more frustrating than having lofty expectations of what a museum can offer a child and then being let down by the actual offerings. Parents do not want this to happen, and as a museum professional, you certainly do not want frustrated parents leaving negative reviews or sharing their disappointment with fellow parents. This can be avoided by being open, honest, and upfront with parents when approached in person and in all of your marketing campaigns. This degree of honesty will make the facility appear trustworthy in the eyes of the millennial parent.

An even bigger issue, and one I suspect will become a topic at the forefront of the discussions surrounding museums and accessibility in the near future, is how museums are working to make their facilities more pleasurable and accessible for children with developmental and intellectual disabilities. According to the Center for Disease Control, today 1 in 59 children will be diagnosed with autism.[11] As millennials are currently the largest generation in existence and the age group most likely to be parents at this time, this diagnosis and others like it will enter in to their decision-making processes when choosing recreational activities for their children. The museum of tomorrow needs to be staffed with people who see this impending future and are making great strides to institute those needed accommodations.

> **Textbox 5.3**
>
> "When I take my son (who has autism) to a museum, I first look for some place where, if necessary, I can take him to decompress . . . having a quiet place to go, where he can regroup, is something that makes the experience better for everyone." —Anna Tozzi Barbay, 35

There are institutions which have already begun working tirelessly to create safe spaces for children with autism spectrum disorder and other disabilities. Again, the Mosaic Templars Cultural Center does not disappoint. Of all of the interviews I did as part of my research for this book, this institution was the most forthcoming about how important it is to institute these accommodations and to understand that this is going to be a common experience for the children of tomorrow. Director Christina Shutt spoke passionately about her work within her institution and in conjunction with other organizations such as the Arkansas Arts Council to push for these accommodations to be made and for there to be more research regarding how their museum and others can be more accessible for these individuals in the future.[12] From my viewpoint as a mother of a child with developmental disabilities, the efforts made by the staff at this museum to accommodate children like mine really resonated with me; and with a diagnosis rate that is high and seemingly increasing, there can be no doubt that this will remain a prevalent and important part of the discussion of museums and accessibility moving forward.

> **Textbox 5.4**
>
> ### DID YOU KNOW?
>
> According to researchers, 1 in 59 children born today will be diagnosed with Autism Spectrum Disorder. This means your organization needs to be planning to serve this demographic and their mostly millennial parents now and in the future. Visit advocacy websites like www.autismspeaks.org to learn about the diagnosis and to help you create a plan for crafting a more inclusive museum environment. Together, we can be inclusive and accessible.

Christina discussed some of the low and no-cost changes she has instituted at their facility to make their children's programming more accommodating for every type of child. She recognizes that much of the research promotes changes that are costly, like painting all of the walls a neutral color for example, but she is also adamant that changes can be made at a more basic and inexpensive level.[13] The experiences that they offer at the Mosaic Templars Cultural Center for children with intellectual disabilities are twofold: accommodations to promote inclusivity in general children's programming and spectrum-specific programming designed with their needs in mind. To help parents feel more comfortable and see practical tools in place to make their child's experience pleasurable, they use colored duct tape to create paths on the floors to direct the children in their activities. These paths lead to stop signs, which are symbols most children recognize and understand. The activities that are provided are guided and specific to help promote focus. The events for children on the spectrum are themed to an activity, such as photography, and are advertised as specifically offered for children on the spectrum with titles like "Creativity on the Spectrum."[14] Many of the events geared specifically toward children on the spectrum are held before opening hours or when the museum first opens to limit the number of people and distractions. When an activity is planned, sensory needs are always considered. For example, when they made beaded necklaces recently, the staff took the children's sensory issues and dexterity into consideration and provided different types of materials for all ability levels. These programs are offered once monthly and provide a consistent basis for specialized access for children on the spectrum.[15]

In regard to inclusivity, the facility also makes accommodations as they are able. They host a story time once monthly for all children and want every type of child to feel welcome to attend. They recognize that not all children,

---

Textbox 5.5

"We are more than a museum . . . we want to be a safe space for people. For folks who are often marginalized, we want to be able to hold that space for them—and not just for people of color in the community but people with disabilities as well." —Christina Shutt, Director, Mosaic Templars Cultural Center

especially those on the spectrum, are able or willing to sit still for such an event. Their solution is to provide various types of seating, such as bean bags and other chairs, that may make these children more comfortable.[16] Small changes and accommodations like these can drastically change the experiences of the parents of these children and the children themselves. You will never find a more loyal millennial patron than the parent of a child with a disability whom you make feel welcomed; the benefits of this are priceless. It is my hope that more museums will make inclusivity for children with intellectual disabilities a priority in the future. For more information on the Mosaic Templars Cultural Center's accommodations for intellectually disabled children, please see textbox 5.6.

Textbox 5.6

Event Highlight: Creativity on the Spectrum

Facility: Mosaic Templars Cultural Center

Location: Little Rock, Arkansas

Budget: ~$1–2 Million (Large-Mid-sized museum)

Event Description: "MTCC is dedicating the evening of October 11 to bring the museum experience to those with autism. The evening will include a special self-guided tour of the Creativity Arkansas exhibit, 'Treasured Memories: My Life, My Story,' an art program in the museum classroom, with special considerations made to those with sensory processing difficulties. We are dedicated to an #InclusiveArkansas and believe it is important to celebrate the history of the African-American experience in Arkansas with **all** Arkansans! The evening's art activities are targeted towards children and teenagers, but all are welcome to partipate." (Pulled directly from http://www.mosaictemplarscenter.com/Default .aspx?PageID=20869121&A=SearchResult&SearchID=7767673&Object ID=20869121&ObjectType=1)

Attendance: varies, but steady

Primary Ways Marketed: Social media platforms, website

Director's Take: "These events work because we know how necessary it is to ask families for their input. We ask: 'How can we help you? How can we be more welcoming to you and your family?'" —Christina Shutt, Director

Why It Works: Christina and her staff recognize the need for programs that promote inclusivity for children with disabilities, intellectual or otherwise, within their community and work tirelessly to create and offer them. Christina works closely with entities who share these same values and implement those accommodations that fit the facility itself and also fit into their budget. She utilizes everything from comfy bean bag chairs to yellow duct tape and neutral painted walls to create a safe space for children on the spectrum. Involving the families and soliciting their feedback creates a sense of ownership among them towards the facility and makes them loyal patrons.

In summation, creating an accessible museum or cultural institution can be as easy as creating new and user-friendly signage, maintaining an online presence, and putting some tape down on the floor for children with intellectual disabilities. This is simplifying the matter, but the point is this: accessibility is attainable and does not take away from your budget. Museum professionals should understand that without accessibility, the ideas of relevance, uniqueness, and affordability are pointless. Millennials first need to feel welcomed by your facility before they can take the step of deciding if patronizing the facility is cost effective, if the programs are unique, or if the mission is relevant to them. Train your staff, be as honest with potential visitors about the strengths and potential weaknesses of your facility as possible, and do your best to make reasonable accommodations for all visitors. Try to anticipate the needs of visitors by viewing your facility through fresh eyes. Could you find your way if you had never visited before? Did the marketing for the exhibit feel inclusive? Can intellectually or physically disabled individuals participate in meaningful ways at your museum? Questions like these are vital for museum professionals to ponder as they move forward creating a more welcoming and accessible environment for their patrons now and in the future.

NOTES

1. American Alliance of Museums, Facing Change: Insights from AAM's DEAI Working Group, https://www.aam-us.org/wp-content/uploads/2018/04/AAM-DEAI -Working-Group-Full-Report-2018.pdf (accessed February 20, 2019).

2. American Alliance of Museums, Facing Change: Insights from AAM's DEAI Working Group, https://www.aam-us.org/wp-content/uploads/2018/04/AAM-DEAI -Working-Group-Full-Report-2018.pdf (accessed February 20, 2019).

3. Joshua Weinstein (Millennial) in discussion with the author, June 2018.

4. Joshua Weinstein (Millennial) in discussion with the author, June 2018.

5. Joshua Weinstein (Millennial) in discussion with the author, June 2018.

6. Colleen Dilenschneider, "Schedule Drives Visitation to Cultural Organizations and Nobody is Talking About It (DATA) Colleen Dilenschneider," *Know Your Own Bone* (blog), https://www.colleendilen.com/2016/04/06/schedule-is-the-top-influ encer-of-visitation-to-cultural-organizations-and-nobody-is-talking-about-it-data/ (accessed August 30, 2018).

7. "Millennials: Confident. Connected. Open to Change," Pew Research Center, Washington, D.C. (February 24, 2010), accessed December 8, 2017, http://www.pew socialtrends.org/2010/02/24/millennials-confident-connected-open-to-change/.

8. Loretta Mordi, "Why Museums Need to Embrace a Culture of Accessibility— Rereeti—Revitalizing Museums," *Rereeti: Revitalizing Museums* (blog), https://rereeti .wordpress.com/2015/09/09/why-museums-need-to-embrace-a-culture-of-accessibil ity/ (accessed September 1, 2018).

9. Loretta Mordi, "Why Museums Need to Embrace a Culture of Accessibility— Rereeti—Revitalizing Museums," *Rereeti: Revitalizing Museums* (blog), https://rereeti .wordpress.com/2015/09/09/why-museums-need-to-embrace-a-culture-of-accessibil ity/ (accessed September 1, 2018).

10. Marianne Babel, "Sticky History: Connecting Historians with the Public," *The Public Historian* vol. 32, no. 4 (Fall 2010) p. 80.

11. Jon Baio, Lisa Wiggins, Deborah Christensen et al., "Prevalence of Autism Spectrum Disorder Among Children Aged 8 Years—Autism and Developmental Disabilities Monitoring Network, 11 Sites, United States, 2014." MMWR Surveil-lance Summaries 2018, 67 (No. SS-6):1–23. DOI: http://dx.doi.org/10.15585/mmwr .ss6706a1.

12. Christina Shutt (Director Mosaic Templars Cultural Association) in discussion with the author, August 2018.

13. Christina Shutt (Director Mosaic Templars Cultural Association) in discussion with the author, August 2018.

14. "MTCC 'Creativity on the Spectrum' aims for inclusivity," http://www.mosaic templarscenter.com/BlogRetrieve.aspx?PostID=884471&A=SearchResult&SearchID =7745554&ObjectID=884471&ObjectType=55 (accessed August 27, 2018).

15. Christina Shutt (Director Mosaic Templars Cultural Association) in discussion with the author, August 2018.

16. Christina Shutt (Director Mosaic Templars Cultural Association) in discussion with the author, August 2018.

6

Looking Ahead

The Museum of the Future

THIS chapter will discuss what the future of museums will look like with millennials at the helm, in volunteer positions, as staff members, as members, and as regular patrons. First, this chapter will outline what positions millennials currently fill within the museum realm. Second, it will discuss where millennial voices need to be present, but currently are not, as well as where there is room for further involvement. Lastly, this chapter will envision the ideal future relationship between museums and millennials. By the end of this chapter, readers will feel empowered to make changes to their respective institutions that will allow for a more productive and fruitful relationship between the millennial generation and world of museums and cultural institutions.

MILLENNIALS AND MUSEUMS: CURRENT RELATIONSHIP

For the majority of visitors, it probably seems that millennials can be found at most museums on the frontline as front desk attendants, gift shop clerks, gallery assistants, and the minds behind social media campaigns. On the whole, this assertion is true. Millennials are already very involved in the museum world and, as many of my interviewees noted, they are in the ranks of the museum hierarchy as volunteers and staff members. While millennials are often the most visible, they still do not make up the majority of individuals employed by museums and cultural institutions, despite being the largest generation in history and the documented knowledge that millennials are interested in these facilities.

Even further, it is considered unusual to see millennials holding high-ranking positions, such as museum directors or department heads, and even more unusual still to find them in boardrooms and trustees' meetings.

The museum world is struggling to adjust to the level of millennial interest in working for museums and many institutions continue to use volunteer and internship opportunities as the gateway to gainful employment. This opportunity can manifest itself in many ways, such as someone working as a full-time volunteer for years on end, only to be offered a part-time position as a gift shop cashier despite having put in years of dedicated service and a clear loyalty to and interest in the facility. This injustice often happens to millennials with advanced degrees as well, making it difficult for the next generation of college students to determine if going into this field will prove stable in the future. Museum professionals can and should do more to encourage the millennial generation to work for their institutions and provide opportunities for them to make a difference in the museum world while earning a living wage.

While the economy certainly dictates the levels at which many institutions are able to hire, both in number of staff members and in wage, it is important for museum professionals in charge of hiring new team members to be able to entice and engage millennial talent at their institutions. Luckily for those on the hiring end, millennials clearly value purpose over pay, mission over money, and freedom from stagnant work over paid vacation days. Various studies support this notion, including many published in the books already cited in this work.[1] Millennials simply want to save the world, and they expect their jobs to aid them in this endeavor.

According to one source, millennials "choose making a life over making a living."[2] They are "looking for work that is meaningful and fulfilling" and value "the social aspect of work . . . like collaborating closely with, and learning from, colleagues and managers they respect, and hope to form friendships with their coworkers."[3] Millennials place importance on the idea of meaningful work partially because of their collective upbringing, which emphasized participation and inclusion. While it is simply not possible to make sweeping generalizations about an entire generation, studies seem to continuously conclude that millennials truly want to make a difference in the world, and based on the sheer number of millennials we see working full-time hours for places they love for little or no pay, it would seem this conclusion is correct.

One of the primary descriptors used by society to describe the millennial generation is self-absorbed. As we discussed in the first chapter, there are many more, but this particular adjective, or some derivative of it, seems to be the most prevalent; and, for the most part, it is basically true. Millennials do have a certain sense of narcissism about them in that they value what they bring to the table and expect for others to value their talents as well. Narcissism may seem like a personality trait that would make millennials poor employees or advocates for your facility; in fact, narcissism is the trait that makes them some of the most loyal employees in this sector.

Authors Credo, Lanier, Matherine, and Cox describe this positive relationship between the millennial generation and narcissism by stating: "Through participation in organizational activities, narcissists may achieve a positive motivational state of gratification. Similarly, entitled individuals tend to value their own contributions more than others and may validate this self-perception through participation."[4]

This association between narcissism, validation, and participation builds the case that millennials make great volunteers. This same group of authors purport that "research indicates that volunteering and community involvement activity has increased among the younger generation."[5] This "save the world" mentality feeds off millennial narcissism, and turns what is usually viewed as a negative adjective into a positive moniker for the generation. Millennials want to, and more importantly need to, contribute to society to feel whole and to define their own self-worth. Museum professionals would do well to see this personality trait as an asset and continue to value millennials as volunteers at their institutions.

Part of this millennial participation can be seen in the importance they place on learning and development opportunities within the workplace. According to a research study done by Udemy, learning and professional development was listed second only to healthcare on a survey designed to ask millennials the top reasons they decide to work for a company.[6] The survey finds that millennials want "skills training and career development, a healthy and productive work environment, and supportive managers . . . [and] are well aware they have more to learn in order to maintain job performance, and they're prepared to put in the work."[7] This is great news, and also combats the common perception that millennials are lazy. They are not; they simply like to invest in themselves and like to invest their time in workplaces that value that characteristic.

Though it is not as prevalent, millennials can be found currently filling roles in the museum world not only as entry-level employees, but also as mid-level and even some executive-level positions. Millennials are not afraid to put in their time, often as free labor, but do not appreciate being stuck in a position that feels menial and keeps them from doing work they perceive as meaningful. The perception that millennials are changing jobs at a rapid rate and do not have any loyalty to their employers is false; however, it may appear that way in some regards because millennials want positions that help them grow and challenge them by allowing them to engage in different tasks daily.[8] This means that the typical nine-to-five position that keeps them at a desk all day, provides little interaction with visitors or coworkers, or offers the exact same work day in and day out is not appealing to this generation and they are likely to leave those positions in favor of more dynamic work.

In their initial predictions about the millennial generation, Howe and Strauss suggested that millennials will become "civic achievers, institution builders, team players, heroes."[9] These adjectives accurately describe how the millennial generation wishes to be viewed and embodies the characteristics they expect employers to see in them and appreciate in their work. Millennials often seek out companies who think along these same "save the world" lines, such as museums and cultural institutions with educational missions. Millennials wish to work for museums and cultural institutions for many reasons, including that a significant portion of the millennial childhood was spent in passive leisure at places like libraries and museums, so many have a positive connection with these entities.[10] Harkening back to that discussion of relevance and nostalgia in chapter 4, it would make perfect sense that millennials would flock to work for these entities which make them feel safe in a dangerous world. Museums provide a refuge that millennials seek while also offering opportunities to make their mark on the world; it is a recipe for a long-standing and mutually beneficial relationship between millennials and museums.

MILLENNIALS AND MUSEUMS: AREAS FOR IMPROVEMENT

Millennials are living in a world where they are the largest generation at this time. They have a documented interest in arts and culture, and yet, they are still underserved in this arena. Underserved takes many forms. Millennials are not being marketed to as effectively as possible in order to reach the majority of those people interested in visiting cultural sites. Millennials are not being valued as highly for the contributions they make as volunteers and interns, instead being expected to work for little or no pay for extended periods of time.[11] Millennials are rarely seen in the boardroom, and are rarely approached to become a trustee or board member for nonprofits. Millennials are given positions of executive authority, such as directors, at low levels compared to their baby boomer and generation X counterparts. All of these areas must be improved if the museum world is to remain relevant as the newer generation reaches adulthood. Millennials need to be a significant part of the way moving forward.

This entire book has discussed ways in which your institution's staff may be able to rethink and reassess your current and future programming to attract a millennial audience, including marketing to this generation. Those chapters, hopefully, have provided substantial insight into how to move forward with engaging this demographic. What has been discussed less, though, is millennials behind the scenes in the museum world as volunteers, staff members, executives, and board members. I want to focus this discussion here because millennial leadership is vital for achieving a successful level of millennial engagement. Without the millennial voice permeating the ranks of every museum and cultural institution, millennials will continue to be underserved. If that happens, then we as museum professionals are doing a disservice to our communities. We need to incorporate the millennial voice into all aspects of the museum world to ensure it is being heard.

The first major change that needs to occur is to transition from a museum world staffed primarily by unpaid volunteers to recognizing the value in a person's education and rewarding it with paid work. This is not to say we need to rid ourselves of volunteer programs. Volunteer programs are necessary parts of a museum's staff, especially small museums. Some museums would not even exist if not for the dedication of a volunteer staff, mine included. My point here is this: if your institution is not employing educated, full-time staff members, then you are missing an opportunity to grow your museum and make it into the best version of itself. Millennial workers are graduating every year with degrees in fields that can help your museum, yet they are not being invested in by these institutions due to a lack of funding or budgeting constraints. As museum leaders, we need to shift our perspective. Your museum is worth investing in; this means putting money into salaries to find and to retain good people. Millennials just happen to be the best up-and-coming source of capable employees.

This also means investing in millennial salaries based upon their backgrounds and abilities, as well as fair compensation for the cost of living in your area. According to the Bureau of Labor Statistics, average salaries in 2017 generally fell in the lower-middle class column. Curators appeared to be valued higher than both museum technicians and public relations specialists with salary levels reported at $56,480, $41,780, and $51,510 respectively.[12] These numbers appear rather fair at first glance, but when analyzed further, it is apparent that what is a livable salary for someone in Utah is not the same for someone living in New York City. If city officials wish to attract a millennial presence to their areas, the salaries offered to them by museums and other employers need to be reasonable for the cost of living in that area. Without making this change, many areas will continue to see a limited millennial presence in the millennial workforce.

As far as executive leadership, millennials are often qualified for these jobs, but are passed over for more "seasoned" professionals, generally someone older with more years of service in the industry. In many ways, this way of thinking makes perfect sense; however, in a world that is constantly changing in terms of technological innovations and incorporating those technologies into marketing campaigns, museum professionals should note that millennials are likely the most knowledgeable individuals regarding these advances. They grew up alongside technology, and are currently the most well-versed generation in the language of social media, applications, and software. As technology changes and the museum world seeks to incorporate these technologies, millennials should be leading the way.

A common misconception about the generation that likely has kept institutions from placing millennials in these executive roles is that millennials lack interpersonal communication skills, which are replaced in their daily lives with conversations that occur on screens and over messenger applications. There is certainly some truth to this criticism, and many millennials do struggle to make their way as public speakers. Part of the problem is that many are never given the chance to do so, or the platform from which to speak with authority. Millennials possess a fear of failure and often avoid taking risks as a result.[13] This same mentality is associated with public speaking. If millennials were given more opportunity to practice interpersonal skills, perhaps this perception would be replaced with a version of adults capable of giving speeches and crafting relationships with donors.

In one of the interviews I did for this book, a senior management professional mentioned some of the downsides of working with millennials, and I think it is important to include those views here. This person had many wonderful things to say about their many millennial coworkers, but felt compelled to mention some of the difficulties in working with them as well. Much like the idea of narcissism, many of the negative traits this person attributed to millennial workers are valid. This interviewee began by describing the millennials with whom they worked as energetic and full of ideas, but soon added that it was noticeable that many lacked interpersonal communication skills. There had even been instances when complaints were made by the public and by other employees regarding millennial staff because of their lack of decorum in holding conversations. Some millennial employees were reported to have used the technology at their fingertips as literal barriers between themselves and the guests, making them feel uncomfortable and rarely looking up to greet them.[14] Of course, I think everyone can agree that we see these behaviors in public every day; however, is this issue just indicative of a millennial workforce? As our society grows into one that is ever reliant on technology and handheld devices, it is likely this trend is one that is spread across most generations; but because millennials are often those part-time workers on the front lines, we as patrons see them more prevalently exhibiting these unacceptable behaviors.

The other areas in which the interviewee noted deficits regarding millennial employees were centered around the idea of a fear of failure. This person stated that many resented being corrected, were unable to take constructive criticism, and held grudges as a result. Furthermore, they did not react well when their ideas were not implemented.[15] This is certainly a millennial characteristic based in that fear of failure instilled in the generation from childhood. For millennials, it sometimes seems that nothing short of exceptional work is failure. Millennials aspire to perfection, and resent being classified as "less than" or second best. There are definite childhood roots here.

At this point in the interview I had to ask: were college museum studies programs adequately preparing millennials and subsequent generations to be successful in these kinds of workplace environments? The interviewee had some experience here as someone behind the scenes who had participated in conversations about this exact subject. We both agreed that the truthful answer was maybe not.[16] Many college programs create within students an inflated expectation of what museum environments are like across the board. College instructors and museum professionals need to work together to ensure that the next round of museum studies graduates understand that all museums are not created equal. They do not all have "lab perfect" environments with climate control and a staff person for every task. Perhaps many millennials were given this mistaken impression that, as museum studies graduates, they would all be given jobs at facilities that could help them produce their visions of grandeur. Many may not have been prepared to work for facilities without those climate-controlled archives, well-equipped processing rooms, large budgets, computers for every staff member, and other amenities. The solution is likely a simple one: change the narrative used in the classroom and provide students with insight into what life is like in small and mid-sized museums for recent graduates. By focusing on teaching students how to make do and find creative solutions for institutions with limited funding and staff, instructors would be preparing them for the real-world museums inhabit and allow these students to be better prepared for the museum workforce.

Indeed, millennials have their flaws as all people in all generations do, but I am advocating that their negative personality traits can often be used for the benefit of the museum world. With the right training and opportunity for growth, millennials can become some of the most loyal staff members at your museum or cultural institution. They simply need to be afforded the chance to prove themselves through a livable wage, not an unceasing thread of paid and unpaid internships. If you place value on their time and talents, they will put their time and talents to work for your institution.

MILLENNIALS AND MUSEUMS: AN IDEAL FUTURE

When I close my eyes and imagine an ideal museum world, I see the picture set before you: a boardroom filled with people of every size, shape, color, background, ability level, sexual orientation, parental status, and age group. For how can we be an inclusive world meant for the enjoyment of all, if all are not given a voice in how we operate? Millennials will play a key role as this idyllic world comes into existence. I firmly believe it will.

FIGURE 6.1
Finally Indeed
Created for Publication by Morven Moeller, 2018

First, we have reason to celebrate as museum professionals. Millennials like and value museums and cultural institutions. They see them as worthy of their time, money, and efforts. They equate them with avenues for social justice and worldwide movements for the greater good. Museums are viewed as trustworthy places from which millennials can gather information. Millennials and the museum world are set up for a prosperous future relationship.

I predict that as many millennials begin to reach the age of eligibility to serve in the political arena, we may see a surge in advocacy for museums, cultural centers, and for the humanities in general. Millennials may be known most widely for their technological prowess, but many still hold the humanities dear to their hearts. As millennials begin to serve in local governments, congress, and lobbying groups, they will be at the center of the decision-making process for allocating funds to the humanities. Many of those museums and cultural institutions which rely on government funding for general operations should take notice of this likely future, and spend time now fostering positive relationships with a millennial audience. If all goes well, millennials will be at the forefront of a fully funded humanities sector in this country within the next few decades.

With their love for supporting noble causes, millennials are also likely to become the next generation of small business owners and nonprofit leaders. Therefore, millennials will be vital resources for potential partnerships with your museums. They will be the people you will need to befriend to help you in creating programming that will incorporate the community and reach larger audiences. They will also be your best advocates, since they are a generation known for readily sharing their opinions on social media and otherwise. Museum professionals will continue to be able to capitalize on this fact in the future as millennials work alongside them to promote those museums and other causes they deem worthy. The relationships you cultivate with millennials now will continue to be valid for many decades to come, and might even save your museum from failing in the future.

As patrons, millennials will continue to be interested in museums and cultural institutions, but will need to be better served. Ultimately, this means they need to see themselves reflected in the museum world as volunteers, staff members, on boards, and in marketing efforts. Millennials will respond better to facilities that make a concerted effort to welcome them wholeheartedly into the fold and make their appreciation of the generation, and its diversity, known. Millennials should continue to be offered volunteer and internship positions, but only as long as it serves both the millennial and the institution. When a millennial has proven his or her dedication to the facility and a position becomes available, museum hiring committees should consider hiring from within and rewarding this kind of loyal service. This will likely lead to less staff turnover and a more dedicated workforce who feel invested in the success of the facility. This is applicable to all generations, but it will be notably appreciated by the millennials.

Millennials must be present in the boardroom of every cultural organization in the future, and not just millennials in general but an ethnically diverse representation of the millennial generation. This is imperative. Why? In part, this needs to happen to ensure their voices are heard; however, the most important reason millennials need to be in the boardroom is so they can have a vested interest in what happens at the facility. Similar to participation in the government, millennials cannot complain about a lack of options geared toward them if they are not actively participating. The question is, why are they not currently seen in the boardrooms of museums across America? There is the obvious reason that many may be perceived as too young or having too little experience, but this idea is not the only reason. Perhaps millennials view boards and board service differently than their elders. Along with board service also comes a financial commitment, and with the financial barriers we discussed in chapters 1 and 2, it is obvious why the millennial purse might be too small for large investments. Colleen Dilenschneider suggests that we need to change the perception of the financial commitment from one of duty to contribution to a worthy cause.[17] Karaugh Brown, Senior Manager of Membership and Patrons at the Guggenheim, also supports this notion, stating in an article that "they don't want to just write a check . . . they want to be part of the process."[18] Millennials want to be involved and see where their contributions are going as both board members and donors.

This would be more likely to align with millennial ideals and bring in more potential board members. I do not think the answer is that millennials are not being invited. Many museum professionals understand that it would be beneficial to have millennials in their corner if they are trying to engage them. Really, the answer remains a mystery, and one that museum professionals will need to continue to explore. Millennials should serve as board members in order to create the idyllic museum of the future.

Finally, millennial senior leadership is key to the future success of museums and cultural institutions. Museum hiring committees must remain blind to a person's age and judge them solely by their abilities. Museum hiring committees need to embrace the young faces of the millennial generation and feel comfortable placing them in high-ranking positions when their work experience and education qualifies them. We as museum professionals set aside the

---

Textbox 6.1

"Being on a board is one of the most deeply rewarding and valuable things I have ever been a part of; however, I don't know many other millennials who are on the board of a visitor-serving organization."
—Colleen Dilenschneider, Chief Market Engagement Officer, IMPACTS Research and Development

---

prejudices we have come to believe about this generation in favor of judging them by their accomplishments. Millennials can and do make superb senior museum professionals, and in the future, they should be placed in these positions and lead the museum world into new and exciting territory.

I cannot end this conversation without insight from Colleen Dilenschneider, who has been frequently referenced in this work and is arguably one of the foremost experts on millennial engagement with cultural entities. I was afforded the opportunity to interview her directly for this book, and am delighted to say she is just as knowledgeable in real life as she is on her blog *Know Your Own Bone*. When I asked her how she envisioned the future of museums, she took a deep breath and let out a long sigh. "Gosh, that is quite the question," she said, "there's just so much to say."[19] Indeed, there is so much to say. While this book focuses on how to create, incorporate, revise, and implement programs for millennials, programming is obviously not the one and only answer to engaging millennials. Colleen stated:

> By focusing only on programming, museums give off this vibe that we are not always for millennials, but are for millennials only during certain special times. We need to shift the perspective. We need to utilize those events to underscore how awesome the museum is ALL of the time. We, as an industry, tend to over-program because we either forget or cannot recognize the permanent collection as something that is always fun to visit. We need to focus our efforts there, because millennial talk is really everybody talk.[20]

This concept that millennial talk is everybody talk is one Colleen frequently purports in her articles and in trainings and talks she gives for industry leaders. Her company has done numerous studies to suggest that millennials are really just like everyone else when it comes to engagement, since technology is now so commonplace and part of almost everyone's everyday life. She stated that we often attribute transparency, personalization, integrity, and social progress to millennials only and define this as millennial talk, but what these ideas really are is talk about how the internet is changing the motivations, expectations, and behaviors for cultural organizations in general for all generations.[21] In reality, she is right. All that really separates millennials from other generations is the date range in which they were born; yet, it is also true that their childhoods have informed how they make decisions as adults, and as we have seen throughout the chapters of this book, it also informs what programs they value and are likely to attend. Millennials like to view themselves as special, and expect the institutions they patronize to single them out as well.

The museum of the future must include millennials, and every other generation, in all aspects of its operations. Millennials need to be patrons, behind the scenes, at the front desk, in the boardroom, lobbying for the humanities, advocating for funding and inclusion on capitol hill, and serving as senior managers, store clerks, volunteers, interns, and in every other nook and cranny of the museum world. It is time for museum professionals to take the issue of millennial engagement by the horns and implement new strategies at their respective facilities to ensure a long and fruitful relationship with the coveted patron generation.

Now, let's get started.

NOTES

1. For reference, see Sustainable Brands, "3/4 of Millennials Would Take a Pay Cut to Work for a Socially Responsible Company I Sustainable Brands," https://www.sustainablebrands.com/news_and_views/organizational_change/sustainable_brands/34_millennials_would_take_pay_cut_work_socia.

2. Eddy S. W. Ng, Linda Schweitzer, and Sean T. Lyons, "New Generation, Great Expectations," *Journal of Business and Psychology* 25, no. 2, Special Issue: "Millennials and the World of Work: What You Didn't Know You Didn't Know" (June 2010): 282, http://www.jstor.org/stable/40605786.

3. Ng, Schweitzer, and Lyons, "New Generation, Great Expectations," 283.

4. Keith R. Credo, Patricia A. Lanier, Curtis F. Matherine III, and Susie S. Cox, "Narcissism and Entitlement in Millennials: The Mediating Influence of Community Service Self Efficacy on Engagement," *Personal and Individual Differences* 101 (2016): 193, http://dx.doi.org/10.1016/j.paid.2016.05.370.

5. Credo, Lanier, Matherine, and Cox, "Narcissism and Entitlement in Millennials: The Mediating Influence of Community Service Self Efficacy on Engagement," 193.

6. Udemy, "Udemy in Depth: 2018 Millennials at Work Report," https://research .udemy.com/wp-content/uploads/2018/06/Udemy_2018_Measuring_Millennials_ Report_20180618.pdf (accessed March 7, 2019).

7. Udemy, "Udemy in Depth: 2018 Millennials at Work Report," https://research .udemy.com/wp-content/uploads/2018/06/Udemy_2018_Measuring_Millennials_ Report_20180618.pdf (accessed March 7, 2019).

8. Sara D. Smith and Quinn Galbraith, "Motivating Millennials: Improving Practices in Recruiting, Retaining, and Motivating Younger Library Staff," *The Journal of Academic Librarianship* 38 (2012): 139.

9. Neil Howe and William Strauss, *Millennials Rising: The Next Great Generation.* New York: Vintage Books, 2000, 66.

10. Howe and Strauss, *Millennials Rising*, 173.

11. For an accurate snapshot of the relationship between millennials and internships, see Alex William's *New York Times* article, "For Interns, All Work and No Payoff" at https://www.nytimes.com/2014/02/16/fashion/millennials-internships.html.

12. Bureau of Labor Statistics, "Industries at a Glance: Museums, Historical Sites, and Similar Institutions: NAICS 712," http://www.bls.gov/iag/tgs/iag712.htm (accessed March 9, 2019).

13. Howe and Strauss, *Millennials Rising*, 185.

14. Anonymous Museum Professional in discussion with the author, July 2018.

15. Anonymous Museum Professional in discussion with the author, July 2018.

16. Anonymous Museum Professional in discussion with the author, July 2018.

17. Colleen Dilenschneider (Chief Market Engagement Officer, IMPACTS Research and Development) in discussion with the author, August 2018. For more information on Colleen's work, please see her blog at https://www.colleendilen.com/.

18. Michael Cannell, "The Millennial Museum," American Alliance of Museums, 2016 http://labs.aam-us.org/buildingculturalaudiences/the-millennial-museum/ (accessed March 7, 2019).

19. Colleen Dilenschneider (Chief Market Engagement Officer, IMPACTS Research and Development) in discussion with the author, August 2018.

20. Colleen Dilenschneider (Chief Market Engagement Officer, IMPACTS Research and Development) in discussion with the author, August 2018.

21. Colleen Dilenschneider (Chief Market Engagement Officer, IMPACTS Research and Development) in discussion with the author, August 2018.

Appendix

Museums and Millennials *Interview Questions (for Millennials)*

1. Please state your name, birth year, and age.
2. When you hear the word "millennial," what comes to mind?
3. Would you say you identify as a millennial? Why or why not?
4. What are some of your favorite museums? Why?
5. When choosing how to spend your free time, what factors do you consider?
6. How often do you visit museums?
7. Do you primarily visit museums to tour the facility, see special exhibits, or attend special programs?
8. Can you name a specific special event you attended that you loved? Why?
9. Can you name a specific event that you hated? Why?
10. How much do you factor in the following when choosing to attend events at museums?

    a. Cost of the event
    b. Value of the event
    c. If friends are going
    d. Location
    e. If there are food/refreshments
    f. Content of the programming
    g. Forms of payment accepted

11. If you could put on an event at a museum, what would it be?

12. What do you think museums do wrong when trying to attract a millennial audience?

13. Do you currently serve as a volunteer anywhere?

14. Do you volunteer for a museum? If yes, how did you get started? If no, why not and would you consider doing so in the future?

15. Agree or disagree with the following statement: Millennials value experiences over products.

16. Agree or disagree with the following statement: I am more likely to attend a museum event if alcohol is served.

17. Please provide any comments you think would be useful.

MUSEUMS AND MILLENNIALS INTERVIEW QUESTIONS (FOR MUSEUM EMPLOYEES)

1. What is your name, the name of your museum, and your position? Are you a millennial?

2. What is the primary audience for your museum?

3. What is your average yearly visitation?

4. Are you considered a small museum (yearly budget under $200,000)? If not, would you say you are a medium or large museum?

5. Please provide the mission statement for your museum.

6. When you hear the term "millennial," what comes to mind?

7. Do you have programming geared specifically toward millennials?

8. Which programs put on by your facility have been successful in attracting millennials? Please explain the event, including cost, content, attendance numbers, and how it was marketed if applicable. Is this a recurring event?

9. Which programs have you tried to put on to attract millennials that have proven unsuccessful? Define that lack of success. What do you think went wrong?

10. Do you believe the use of technology is necessary to attract millennials? Explain.

11. What days of the week and times of day do you typically offer events? Is there a specific day/time that seems to work best for your facility?

12. Does your museum charge admission? If so, how much?

13. If you usually charge admission, do you see surges in millennial attendance when you offer open houses or free admission days?

14. Do you have staff members or volunteers at your facility that are millennials? If so, how many and in what capacity do they serve?

15. If you have a museum membership program, what percentage of that membership is made up of millennials?

16. Would you say the children's programming offered by your museum is relevant to millennial parents? Why or why not?

17. Agree or disagree with this statement: Events where alcohol is served provide the foundation for millennial attendance at museums.

18. Agree or disagree with this statement: Millennials value cost of admission over content.

19. Agree or disagree with this statement: Millennials value experiences over products.

20. Agree or disagree with this statement: Millennials want programming geared specifically toward their values.

21. Please provide any further insight into how your museum attracts millennials, the problems faced in marketing to them, and how museums in general can improve reaching this audience.

Index

Page references for figures are italicized

About the Author

Jaclyn Spainhour is a proud millennial and the Director of the Hunter House Victorian Museum in Norfolk, Virginia. A graduate of Old Dominion University, Jaclyn spent time as an adjunct instructor of history at both her alma mater and Tidewater Community College. She serves on the Board of Directors of the Victorian Society in America as the Chair of its Book Awards Committee and the copy editor of the society's journal, *19th Century*. Jaclyn was chosen by the Virginia Association of Museums as a Leadership and Advocacy Fellow for 2019, wherein she will develop a webinar focused on the relationship between autism spectrum disorder and inclusivity in the museum world. Her first publication *Gilded Age Norfolk, Virginia: Tidewater Wealth, Industry, and Propriety* was published in 2015 and serves as a local history text highlighting the importance of the Hunter House Victorian Museum in the local historical landscape.